Barack Obama

Barack
Obama

Stephen Krensky

DK PUBLISHING

LONDON, NEW YORK, MUNICH,
MELBOURNE, AND DELHI

Editor : Beth Landis Hester
Publishing Director : Beth Sutinis
Designer : Mark Johnson Davies
Managing Art Editor : Michelle Baxter
Production Controller : Erika Pepe
DTP Coordinator : Kathy Farias
Photo Research : Anne Burns Images

First American Edition, 2010

10 11 12 13 14 10 9 8 7 6 5 4 3 2 1
Published in the United States
by DK Publishing
375 Hudson Street
New York, New York 10014

DK books are available at special discounts
when purchased in bulk for sales promotions,
premiums, fund-raising,
or educational use. For details, contact:

DK Publishing Special Markets
375 Hudson Street
New York, New York 10014
SpecialSales@dk.com

A catalog record for this book is available
from the Library of Congress.

ISBN 978-0-7566-5805-2 (Paperback)
ISBN 978-0-7566-5804-5 (Hardcover)

Printed and bound in China
by South China Printing Co., Ltd.

Discover more at
www.dk.com

Contents

chapter 1

Hawaiian Beginnings

The year 1961 saw a new president, John F. Kennedy, moving into the White House. At 43, he was the youngest person ever elected to that office. He was also the first to be born in the 20th century. "Let the word go forth from this time and place, to friend and foe alike," Kennedy said at his inauguration, "that the torch has been passed to a new generation of Americans . . . unwilling to witness or permit the slow undoing of those human rights to which this nation has always been committed,

John F. Kennedy took the oath of office on January 20, 1961, becoming the 35th president of the United States.

and to which we are committed today at home and around the world."

Among those rights was supposed to be equality of all kinds—including racial equality. The United States had formally abolished slavery almost 100 years earlier after the end of the Civil War. But banishing slavery did not erase the bigotry against African-Americans. It only changed its name. Legal prejudice soon appeared in many state laws. New rules proclaimed that people couldn't vote if they were poor or didn't own any land. And who were these people mostly? They were black—former slaves and their children who could barely make ends meet.

The prejudice against African-Americans didn't stop with voting. Other laws specifically banned "colored" people from certain hotels and restaurants. They were prohibited from using public drinking fountains and restrooms. Many professional jobs and occupations were closed to them as well.

Was there opposition to these actions? Certainly. But far too often, people, especially white people, looked away

Civil Rights Movement

In the first part of the 20th century, race relations in the United States were marked by inequality. The civil rights movement was a dedicated effort led by black leaders, particularly from 1955 to 1965, to focus attention on racial inequalities and institute meaningful improvements. These efforts helped lead to the landmark Civil Rights Act of 1964, which struck down legal racial segregation in the United States.

SEGREGATION

Segregation is a policy of giving people of specific races different social and economic rights under the law.

rather than confront these injustices. And in some parts of the country, a black person who didn't keep his place, who complained too loudly, might just disappear in the middle of the night and never be heard from again.

Progress, when it came, was slow, painful, and sometimes dangerous. As late as 1955, an African-American secretary named Rosa Parks was arrested in Montgomery, Alabama. What was her crime? She had refused to give up her seat on a bus so that a white passenger could sit down. This one act led to a series of protests, and finally to some long-overdue changes.

Still, in the same year President Kennedy took office, violence erupted on public buses as riders tested new anti-segregation laws. One bus carrying black and white riders was firebombed in Alabama. Elsewhere in the South, angry mobs attacked civil rights activists who insisted on crossing long-established social and cultural lines. While the Reverend Martin Luther King, Jr., a national black leader of the civil rights movement, preached change through peaceful resistance, not everyone shared his views.

Far away from all this turmoil, a baby was born in Honolulu, on the Hawaiian island of Oahu. The date was August 4, 1961. The

"Now is the time to make justice a reality."

–Martin Luther King, Jr.

Martin Luther King, Jr.
(1929–1968)

Dr. Martin Luther King, Jr., was an inspirational leader in the fight for civil rights during the 1950s and 1960s. He was known for using civil disobedience—nonviolent demonstrations—to draw attention to the cause. His famous "I Have a Dream" speech was given in Washington on August 28, 1963, in front of the Lincoln Memorial. Its theme was hope for a time when blacks and whites would live in harmony.

name he was given was the same as his father's—Barack Hussein Obama.

That baby Barack was born at all was somewhat unlikely. His father, Barack Sr., was a young African man from Kenya attending the University of Hawaii. The baby's mother, Ann, was another student at the university, whose family lived in Honolulu.

Barack Obama, Sr., had been born in 1936. He grew up in Kenya in a small village near Lake Victoria. His own father came from a family of prominent farmers. Barack had spent his boyhood going to the local schools and tending his father's goats in his spare time. His intelligence impressed his family and teachers early on, and he was encouraged to pursue his studies in the Kenyan capital of Nairobi. Along the way, he got married in a tribal ceremony at the age of 18 and had two children with his first wife, Kezia.

Two American teachers helped Barack Sr. get a scholarship that allowed him to continue his studies in the United States. Leaving his wife behind, he enthusiastically took this opportunity. He arrived at the University of Hawaii in 1959, the first African student ever to enroll there. Some young men would have been intimidated in such a situation. But not Barack. Twenty-three years old and brimming with confidence, he studied economics and was popular with his classmates.

But while Barack moved easily in his new surroundings, he was keenly aware of the difficulties of arriving in a new country with no friends or family. So he helped create the International Student Association, an organization to help foreign students meet one another. Then he became its first president. He met Ann Dunham in a Russian language course. She was as shy as he was bold, but still she was drawn to the intense young man from abroad. Born in Kansas in 1942, she had been named Stanley Ann

Barack Obama, Sr., was an ambitious young man who worked for the government in Kenya after completing his education in America.

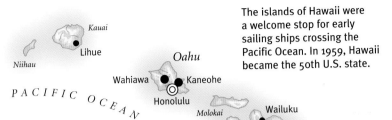

The islands of Hawaii were a welcome stop for early sailing ships crossing the Pacific Ocean. In 1959, Hawaii became the 50th U.S. state.

Kauai

Lihue

Niihau

PACIFIC OCEAN

Oahu

Wahiawa • • Kaneohe
◎ Honolulu

Molokai

Wailuku •

Lanai

Kahoolawe

Maui

Hawaii

• Hilo

because her father, Stanley, had so stubbornly wanted a boy. Ann, as she not surprisingly chose to be called, had lived in California, Texas, and Washington—moving wherever her father's jobs as a furniture salesman took her and her mother, Madelyn. In 1960, after she graduated from high school, the family moved to Hawaii.

The islands looked like a paradise, but they had their own troubled history. The native Hawaiians had been taken advantage of through broken promises and treaties ever since the British captain James Cook first arrived there in 1778. Later, American companies had seized large areas of rich agricultural land to grow sugar and pineapples. More recently, plantation owners had started exploiting Asian immigrant workers, who spent 12-hour days toiling in the fields.

Although racial relations were generally more peaceful in Hawaii than in other parts of the United States, Barack and Ann's romance was still unusual. A black man holding hands with a white woman was not a common sight, to

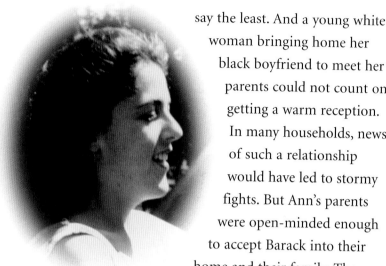

say the least. And a young white woman bringing home her black boyfriend to meet her parents could not count on getting a warm reception. In many households, news of such a relationship would have led to stormy fights. But Ann's parents were open-minded enough to accept Barack into their home and their family. They might have doubted the wisdom of the marriage, given Ann's youth and inexperience, but they believed she was old enough to make her own decisions.

Ann Dunham fell in love with Barack Obama, Sr., without worrying about what other people would think of them as a couple.

The fact that Barack and Ann could marry at all was another thing they couldn't take for granted. Many states had laws forbidding miscegenation—the marriage of two people from different races. And in such places, the news that Ann was pregnant with Barack's baby would be considered even worse. In parts of the country, a black man daring to date— let alone marry—a white woman might have been harmed or even killed by people determined to keep different races separate. Even in places where violence was unlikely, mixed-race couples were made to feel different, unwelcome, and unworthy of such blessings as marriage or parenthood.

Luckily, Hawaii was thousands of miles and a wide ocean away from such practices. And so young Barack, or Barry as he was called, began life happily unaware of these controversies. As he later wrote, "That my father looked nothing like the people around me—that he was black as pitch, my mother white as milk—barely registered in my mind."

The intense, beautiful memories of those times stuck with him. Years later, he could still "retrace the first steps I took as a child and be stunned by the beauty of the islands. The trembling blue plane of the Pacific. The moss-covered cliffs and the cool rush of Manoa Falls, with its ginger blossoms and high canopies filled with the sound of invisible birds. The North Shore's thunderous waves, crumbling as if in a slow-motion reel. The shadows off Pali's peaks; the sultry, scented air."

As a small boy, little Barack loved to play in the Hawaiian surf.

For a small toddler taking his first steps, it was absolutely perfect.

chapter 2

An Unsettled Boyhood

Unfortunately, these pleasant family days were coming to an end. In 1962, Barry's father received an offer of graduate work at Harvard University in Cambridge, Massachusetts. This was exciting news for Barack Sr., who was eager to continue his education. However, the offer only provided enough money for him to make the trip by himself. (Another offer from a school in New York would have allowed Ann and Barry to go, too, but Barack decided that Harvard was the better match for his career.)

Harvard University, founded in 1636, has an international reputation as one of the best universities in the world.

Reluctantly, Ann agreed to the 5,000-mile (8,000-km) separation.

She and Barry would stay behind with her parents. And she would return to college, which she had left when her baby was born.

As things turned out, Barack had no money to travel back to Hawaii for holidays or vacations. Letters passed back and forth between him and Ann, but that wasn't enough to maintain their relationship. The great distance doomed their

Barack often found a comfortable place at the beach to sit with his grandfather Stanley.

marriage, and two years later they were divorced. There was no anger on either side, though Ann at least was disappointed the marriage had not turned out better. Barack seemed less troubled about it. A year later, he returned to Kenya, taking with him both his degree and a young woman, Ruth Nidesand, who would soon become his third wife.

Young Barry knew nothing of all this at the time. At home, his mother and grandmother, whom he called Toot (after the Hawaiian word "Tutu" meaning grandmother), took care of him. He spent his days playing outside, often accompanying his grandfather to the beach or the park.

Among the locals, nobody paid attention to the white grandfather and his black grandson. However, tourists sometimes took more notice of the difference, and would point or make remarks. Stanley Dunham usually ignored them. As far as he was concerned, their prejudice was their problem, not his.

Before long, Barry was introduced to a new man in his mother's life. This was Lolo Soetoro, a visiting student from Indonesia. Lolo's father and oldest brother had been killed during the conflict between the native Indonesians and the Dutch. In the late 1940s, Indonesians had been trying to win their independence, and the Dutch, who had ruled Indonesia for several hundred years, had been resisting. Lolo's mother saved his life after the Dutch army burned their home. Later, she traded her jewelry for food to keep her family alive in the countryside.

Without Barack Sr. around, Barry enjoyed spending time with Lolo. They would wrestle together, and Lolo would tell stories about Indonesia. When his mother told him that she and Lolo were going to get married, Barry didn't mind at all.

In 1966, Lolo got unhappy news from home. Following the latest political upheaval, all Indonesian students studying abroad were being recalled. Lolo had to leave at once. When it became clear that he would be unable to return to Hawaii any time soon, Ann made plans for Barry and her to follow him.

Indonesian Independence

 After years of struggle, the Indonesians finally gained their independence in 1949. But internal strife in the new government created problems for many years to come.

Indonesia was a new world for both mother and son. They were used to the eight main islands of Hawaii, which were only a few hundred miles apart from one end to the other. But Indonesia was made up of more than 17,000 islands, which stretched out for thousands of miles. Hawaii

Indonesia was settled more than 4,000 years ago, but was more recently influenced by several hundred years of Dutch colonialism.

had a population of about one million people, including the tourists. Indonesia's 109 million people ranked it as the fifth most populous nation in the world, behind only China, India, the United States, and Russia.

The capital of Indonesia, Jakarta, made a strong first impression on Barry. It was "a sleepy backwater," he wrote later, with low buildings, rickshaws being pulled along dirt roads, and people shopping in open-air markets. Near his new home, the road was clogged with cars and overcrowded buses. At the house itself, Barry found all kinds of animals, including chickens, ducks, birds of paradise, a cockatoo, and two baby crocodiles.

The architecture in the city of Jakarta reflected the influence of Dutch colonial rule.

He watched one of the chickens being killed for dinner, something he had never

seen in Hawaii. There were other new eating experiences as well. Barry learned to eat raw green chili peppers as well as "dog meat (tough), snake meat (tougher) and roasted grasshopper (crunchy)."

> *"One day soon, [Lolo] promised, he would bring home a piece of tiger meat for us to share."*
>
> –Barack Obama, about his culinary adventures in Indonesia

As best he could, Lolo treated Barry like his own son. One day Barry came home with a lump on his head. It was not his fault, Barry explained. A boy had run off with his friend's soccer ball, and Barry had chased him. The boy had then picked up a rock and thrown it at him. How could he do that, Barry wondered. It was like cheating.

That was not important, Lolo insisted. What mattered was that a young man be able to defend himself. The next day, Lolo came home with boxing gloves and taught Barry to box. "Keep your ends up," he explained. He showed Barry the proper way to stand and where to put his elbows. "You want to keep moving, but always stay low—don't give them a target."

Indonesia is home to many colorful birds, including about 85 different kinds of parrots.

These lessons were important to Lolo. Throughout his life, he had seen people die when they were weak. He had learned that being strong could mean power and protection. "If you can't be strong, be clever and make peace with someone who's strong," Lolo told Barry. "But always better to be strong yourself. Always."

Learning self-defense was only one of Barry's activities. He studied Indonesia's languages and customs. (The people of Indonesia collectively speak more than 700 languages.) He also made friends with other children. Together, Barry and his companions explored the city and its amazing sites, sounds, and flavors: finding odd jobs to make money, chasing crickets and chickens, joining in kite-flying competitions, spying on water buffalo, making shadow puppets, and eating sweet treats from the city's street vendors. They were years he would later remember as "a joyous time, full of adventure and mystery."

Lolo, a geologist, was working for the army when Ann and Barry arrived. His position did not pay well, and even after Ann got a job teaching English to Indonesian businessmen at the American embassy, the family only had money for the basics. But when Lolo was discharged from the army, he found a job with an American oil company. The higher salary allowed the family to move to a bigger

> *"Always better to be strong yourself. Always."*
>
> –Lolo Soetoro

The Soetoro family—Lolo, Ann, Barack, and Maya—pose for a family picture not long after Maya was born.

house with modern conveniences such as a refrigerator and a television set. In 1970, Lolo and Ann had a baby girl, which gave Barry a new half-sister named Maya.

Unfortunately, not everyone was as lucky as the Soetoros. There were beggars in the streets, and sometimes they came knocking at the door. Barry wrote to his grandparents regularly, but he never told them about some of the more upsetting things he experienced—such as "the face of the man who had come to our door one day with a gaping hole where his nose should have been: the whistling sound he made as he asked my mother for food."

Even having a job was no guarantee against poverty. Farmers especially, who relied on the right climate conditions to secure a healthy crop (and enough income to make a living) were vulnerable to unexpected changes in the weather. And the weather was unreliable, at best. Barry saw how the farmers suffered when the crops failed and the dried-out soil crumbled during a season with too little rain. Just as dangerous were the terrible downpours of rain that could flood the streets, wreak havoc on barns and homes, and endanger livestock.

Barry went to school with the local children, but his mother was not satisfied with the education he was receiving there. So she gave him extra lessons in English for three hours every morning before she left for the day. The average eight- or nine-year-old would not look forward to this extra schooling, and Barry was no different. He often protested without success. But his mother remained firm. Barry needed to read and write English as well as any boy raised in America. He could

Indonesian farmers often planted their crops without the benefit of modern machinery or equipment.

grumble all he wanted; he could pretend to be sick. None of that mattered. She wasn't going to change her mind. As she reminded him on many occasions: "This is no picnic for me either, buster."

Looking back later, Barry was grateful for his mother's guidance and high standards. She encouraged him to learn from his new surroundings and find his own way through this new set of customs and circumstances—all of which helped him to be self-sufficient and accept challenges with grace and good manners.

But Ann saw that even with her help, Barry's opportunities in Indonesia would never be as broad as they could be back home in the United States. Barry later recalled, "She knew which side of the divide she wanted her child to be on. I was an American, she decided, and my true life lay elsewhere."

And so it was time to go home.

chapter 3
A Bittersweet Return

Ten-year-old Barry Obama was more than a little nervous. It was his first day at a new school, a place where he knew no one and no one knew him. To make matters worse, Honolulu's Punahou School was not like the schools he was used to. Founded in 1841, it served the bright and well-connected children of Oahu. The well-kept grounds spread across a comfortable landscape of fields and trees.

Although Barry had been born in Hawaii, to his classmates he was just the new kid from Indonesia. Most of them had known one another for years. And they had much in common: similar comfortable houses, similar traditional family lives, similar middle-class

Punahou School is housed in handsome buildings, including this one, on a large campus on Oahu.

wealth. Barry, meanwhile, was now living with his grandparents in their two-bedroom apartment. (His mother

Barry Obama (top row, third from left) smiles happily in this class picture from the fifth grade.

and Maya were still in Indonesia, living with Lolo.)

Nobody at school played soccer or badminton, the sports Barry knew. And he had no clue how to do the things his classmates cared about, like playing football or riding a skateboard. Barry also stood out as one of the few African-Americans enrolled in the school. On his first day, he was asked if his father in Kenya was a cannibal. Certainly not, Barry said. He coolly explained that his father was actually a prince: "My grandfather, see, he's a chief. It's sort of like the king of the tribe, you know . . . like the Indians.

So that makes my father a prince. He'll take over when my grandfather dies."

This was pretty impressive stuff. The other boys naturally wanted to know if Barry planned to someday take the throne for himself. He had to think quickly about that. "Well . . . if I want to, I could. It's sort of complicated, see 'cause the tribe is full of warriors. Like Obama . . . that means 'Burning Spear.' The men in our tribe all want to be chief, so my father has to settle these feuds before I can come."

Although his imagination was hard at work, this was not the first time Barry had fantasized about his father. His mother had shared many stories with him about the Obamas and their ancestors. She told him all about his father's tribe, the Luo, who had migrated to Kenya from the banks of the River Nile.

This view of farmland in Kenya shows a variety of traditional and more modern homes.

"I had visions of ancient Egypt, the great kingdoms I had read about, pyramids and pharaohs, Nefertiti and Cleopatra."

A year later, Barry's mother and his little sister, Maya, returned

> *"I had visions of ancient Egypt, the great kingdoms I had read about, pyramids and pharaohs . . ."*
>
> –Barack Obama, imagining his father's heritage

to Hawaii. Ann had missed her home more than she'd expected, and she wanted both her children to have the advantages of being raised in the United States. Lolo did not come with them, though, because he and Ann had grown apart. So Barry, his mother, and Maya settled into a small apartment near the Punahou campus. Ann enrolled as a graduate student at the University of Hawaii. And Barry's days were busy with school and play and helping out with household chores.

Although his mother was no longer teaching him lessons, she continued on with Barry's moral education. She had strong feelings about the way human beings should treat one another. She "disdained any kind of cruelty or thoughtlessness or abuse of power, whether it expressed itself in the form of racial prejudice or bullying in the schoolyard or workers being underpaid."

Ann also made a point of celebrating the color of Barry's skin. She encouraged him to take pride in his heritage, starting with his father. "You have me to thank for your eyebrows," she told him. "Your father has these little wispy eyebrows that don't amount to much. But your brains, your character, you got from him." Every black person she taught him about was a hero, from Supreme Court justice Thurgood Marshall to actress and singer Lena Horne.

However, it wasn't always easy for Barry to believe everything his mother told him. He once came across an article about a black man who had tried to whiten his skin with chemicals. Why would anyone do this? It made no sense to him. In many ways, his race was still a puzzle he was struggling to understand.

Thurgood Marshall (1908–1993)

Thurgood Marshall was the first African-American justice on the U.S. Supreme Court. When he first applied to law school, he was rejected due to his race. He went on to graduate from Howard University School of Law in 1933. As a lawyer, his most famous case was *Brown v. Board of Education,* which ruled segregation in schools unconstitutional. He served on the Supreme Court from 1967 to 1981.

At this time, Barry's father made an unexpected visit. Barack Sr. had not been back to Hawaii for eight years. After finishing at Harvard, he had started working for the government in Kenya. But at the moment, he was recovering from having been badly injured in a car crash.

Barry and his father share a happy moment during Barack Sr.'s visit to Hawaii.

The visit had its awkward moments. It was hard for Barry to match the vibrant image of his father that his mother had passed along with the actual man who stood before him: "He was much thinner than I expected, the bones of his knees cutting the legs of his trousers in sharp angles: I couldn't imagine him lifting anyone off the ground. Beside him, a cane with a blunt ivory head leaned against the wall. He wore a blue blazer, and a white shirt, and a scarlet ascot. His horn-rimmed glasses reflected the light of the lamp so that I couldn't see his head very well, but when he took the glasses off to rub the bridge of his nose, I saw that they were slightly yellow, the eyes of someone who's had malaria more than once."

Barack Sr. had always been an impatient man, and the passing years had not mellowed him. Even when he showed pride in Barry, his overall manner was not encouraging. He was hard to please. If Barry wasn't working on his homework, he should be. If Barry was working on his homework, he should be working harder. If he was working harder, he should be working harder still.

Barry bristled under such criticism. His mother and grandparents were not pleased, either. Barack had chosen to leave their lives eight years before. He was welcome as a visitor, and he had rights as a father. But that was all. He had given up the privilege of being in charge—whether he saw it that way or not.

Barack had one other important thing on his mind. He wanted Ann, Barry, and Maya to return with him to Africa. Ann refused. In Kenya, Barack already had two wives and six children. It was all perfectly legal, but Ann was not interested in joining such an extensively blended family. And so, when Barack's two-week visit ended, he went home to Africa alone.

A few years later, when Barry was 16, Ann finished her graduate work and made plans to return to Indonesia. She expected Barry to go back with her and Maya. But he said no. "I doubted what Indonesia now had to offer and wearied of being new all over again." And he had an alternative in hand: He had already spoken to his grandparents, and they had agreed that he could live again with them.

Part of the deal with his grandparents was that Barry would cause no trouble. For a typical teenager, of course, this was sometimes easier said than done. Barry went through the same awkward teenage stages as everyone else he knew. His mind and body were both growing, but not always in sync with each other.

Barry's refuge during the next few years was the basketball court. He loved the game "with a consuming passion that would always exceed my limited talent." He spent hours passing balls, taking jump shots, and perfecting a crossover dribble. He went on to play on the Punahou high-school team and even took his game to college gyms, where he picked up lessons that went far beyond the court. He learned that "respect came from what you did and not who your daddy was. . . . That you didn't let anyone sneak up behind you to see emotions—like hurt or fear—that you didn't want them to see."

Having beaten his opponent to the hoop, Barry takes a shot during one of his high-school basketball games.

He became known as "Barry O'Bomber" due to his impressive jump shot. He liked the name and the swagger that went with it. But not everything was as simple as shooting hoops. He was still trying to figure out exactly who he was. He looked like a black student, complete with an Afro hairdo. But living with his white grandparents and knowing the two sides of his heritage made it difficult to settle on an identity.

"As it was, I learned to slip back and forth between my black and white worlds," he later wrote, "understanding that each possessed its own language and customs and structures of meaning." Barry thought that with some effort on his part,

Barry's grandparents, shown here at his high-school graduation, struggled with him as a teenager, but earned his respect and love.

he could make those two worlds come together in a way that made sense. But it seemed impossible to ignore the feeling that his peers saw him as different. It came out in subtle ways—for instance, when white people made a point of saying how much they liked this or that black musician, or assumed he played basketball.

Looking for guidance, Barry turned to the work of black writers—James Baldwin, Ralph Ellison, Langston Hughes, and Richard Wright. Their words—by turn sad, angry, hopeful, and defiant—inspired him. However, they did not provide answers to all his questions. He also tried drinking and drugs, but he found no permanent comfort there, and he recognized the danger of continuing on that path.

All this thinking and experimenting was shaping his personality. Barry developed a rebellious streak, and felt wiser than the adults around him. He invented reasons to argue with his grandparents, just for the fun of it. But by his senior year in high school, Barry had learned that winning arguments with his grandfather because he was better at using words was not so satisfying: "I started to appreciate his need to feel respected in his own house. I realized that abiding by his rules would cost me little, but to him it would mean a lot."

Not that this settled all of his uneasiness. By the time of his high-school graduation, he was aware of how alone he was, being black and not black at the same time. He couldn't shake the feeling that he was on the outside looking in, and he wasn't sure how to deal with it.

On one of her visits home, Barry's mother worried that he had become lazy, more interested in having a good time than working hard. So what if he had, Barry thought? Still, he felt guilty to think that he had genuinely worried or hurt his mother. When he admitted this to her, Ann wasn't surprised. There was no way he could avoid guilt, she explained, because she had "slipped it into your baby food."

By itself, however, guilt couldn't provide enough guidance to lead him. Guilt was more of a warning sign, a light flashing in his head, signaling that he was going in the wrong direction. It was a heads-up he would find useful as life went on.

Barry proudly receives his diploma during the Punahou graduation ceremony in 1979.

chapter **4**

From Coast to Coast

G oing to college in the fall of 1979 was a big step for Barry. He was going to be living away from his family for the first time and also moving to the mainland. He had been accepted at Occidental College in Los Angeles, California. Although California was the closest state to Hawaii, it was still 2,500 miles (4,000 km) of water away.

Occidental College had been founded in 1887. "Oxy," as it was known on campus, was a relatively small place with fewer than 2,000 students. They came from a wide range of ethnic and economic backgrounds.

Barry did not have any particular problems adjusting to life at school. He went to class,

Occidental College was a popular choice for students wishing to attend a private college in Los Angeles.

ate in the dining hall, and hung out with his friends. Most of his spare time was spent outside official college activities. His name did not appear in any Occidental yearbooks or the student newspaper during his time there. He did write some poems that were published in the literary magazine, *Feast*.

One experience that made an impression on Barry in college was meeting other black students whose backgrounds were very different from his. They had grown up in poor neighborhoods where drugs were sold on street corners and gunfire sometimes broke the stillness of the night. These students could rightly claim to be victims of their skin color. Barry, with his white mother and grandparents and middle-class Hawaiian background, could not. And yet, he felt black just as they did—or at least he considered himself to be grouped together with them by the outside world.

He did not have to overcome the obstacles they had already faced. In college, he wrote later, "I had nothing to escape from except my own inner doubt." He felt more like the black students who had lived privileged, suburban lives, seemingly untouched by the urban black experience. These more affluent students felt that they "weren't defined by the color of their skin."

On the other hand, a lot of the young black men and women he met were angry and bitter. They believed the ruling white society had already closed doors to them, doors that would remain shut in the future. If the white man's world would not play fair with them, why should they have

Room 104 of Thorne Hall was Obama's home durnig his time at Occidental.

to live by the white man's rules? Listening to their talk, Barry was drawn into their conflicting emotions. He understood wanting to be part of a world that didn't seem to want him. He felt the pain of not belonging, of having to put on a false front and hide his true self. It seemed like a hopeless situation. And if he could never be accepted as he was—if he would always feel like an outsider—why bother even trying to fit in?

It was a convenient excuse for not living by any rules at all. But some of his black friends had avoided this trap, and they challenged Barry to defend himself: "Who told you that being honest was a white thing?" They asked him. "Who sold you this bill of goods, that your situation exempted you from being thoughtful or diligent or kind, or that morality had a color? You've lost your way, brother." It was time to reevaluate his role in the world—and his responsibilities toward it.

As Barry looked himself over, he saw how much easier it was to sit back and criticize rather than to step forward and make a difference. Around this time, he became involved in the issue of divestment in South Africa. That country enforced a system called apartheid, which made segregation not only legal, but also integral to its society. A black person in South Africa could never rise above a lowly status. The divestment campaign was a plan to get American companies to withdraw financial support from South Africa, in an attempt to force the South African government to change its policies.

At one campus rally, Barry spoke briefly about this issue. The struggle over apartheid, he said "demands that we choose sides. Not between black and white. Not between rich and poor. No—it's a harder choice than that. It's a choice between dignity and servitude. Between fairness and injustice. Between commitment and indifference. A choice between right and wrong . . ."

An End to Apartheid

The practice of apartheid, a government policy of segregation between races, was first instituted in South Africa in 1948 and came to an end in 1994. At that time, the African National Congress won the national elections and came to power. Their first president was 76-year-old Nelson Mandela, who had been imprisoned by the former government for 27 years for his anti-apartheid activities.

The audience was moved. It was a defining moment for Barry, as he realized the power his words could have. He also understood that choosing between right and wrong did not hinge on the issue of color. There was no reason he had to choose between being black or white. He could be both. And in realizing this, he also realized the time had come to leave the name Barry behind. His name was Barack, and he should be proud of it.

The new Barack decided to make a fresh start. He wanted to become part of a larger black community, one that would reflect the richness and diversity of black life. He identified New York City as having such a community, and learning that Occidental College had a transfer-program arrangement with New York's Columbia University, he took advantage of it.

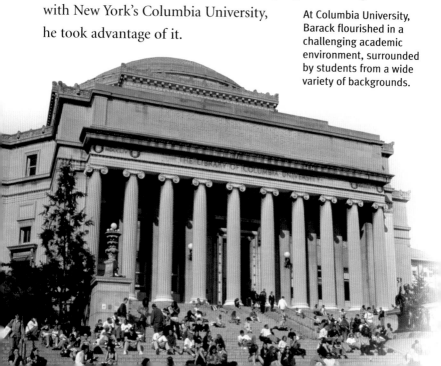

At Columbia University, Barack flourished in a challenging academic environment, surrounded by students from a wide variety of backgrounds.

Columbia University was a far bigger school than Occidental. Founded as King's College in 1754, when New York was still ruled by an English king, it was located in a densely urban section of the city. Both the school and the city were overwhelming in many ways—bigger, grimmer, and more intense than Los Angeles. Barack took months to adjust this new setting. He also became a serious student, learning about social injustice in the classroom and observing it out in the street.

"It's a choice between dignity and servitude. . . . A choice between right and wrong."

–Barack Obama, in a speech at Occidental College

While at Columbia, Barack received some bad news from Kenya: His father had died, killed in a car accident. Though he was only 46, Barack Sr.'s health had been failing for a while. Barack had been planning to visit his father in the near future. Obviously, that would not happen now.

When Barack's mother and sister came to visit him during the summer between his junior and senior years, Ann talked to him at length about his father. She spoke of Barack Sr.'s confidence, how strong-minded he was, at ease in almost every situation. He was very proud, perhaps too proud for his own good. And yet, without that pride, he could never have fueled the ambition to leave home and study abroad.

His father's past continued to occupy Barack's thoughts as he pursued his major (political science with an emphasis

COMMUNITY ORGANIZER

A community organizer works for a nonprofit organization, trying to better the lives of poor people, usually in crowded urban settings.

on international relations). Around the time of his graduation in the spring of 1983, he decided to look for work as a community organizer. This would give him a chance to work in underprivileged settings and try to improve conditions for the people who lived there. "I saw the African-American community becoming more than just the place where you'd been born or the house where you'd been raised," he later wrote. "The community I imagined was still in the making." Most importantly, the work held a promise of redemption, a way to make peace with his mixed heritage.

Barack wrote to every civil rights organization he knew of, and to black officials around the country. He was only looking for an entry-level opening, a place to start—but no one even answered his inquiries. Stymied for the moment, he accepted a more conventional job doing research for a company that assisted American firms operating abroad. The delay was temporary, a bump in the road, he thought.

As the months passed and he started succeeding at work, his views softened. It became tempting to think of building a corporate career, making a lot of money, dressing well, eating well, living well. Money had never meant a lot to Barack. But in a city like New York, where it could make a big difference in the kind of apartment you could rent or the kind of restaurant you could eat in, money certainly came in handy.

What shattered this plan was more news from Kenya. Barack was in touch with his older half sister, Auma. She had been planning to visit New York, to see him for the first time. But then she called with sad news. Their younger half-brother David had been killed in a motorcycle accident—so she wouldn't be coming, not now.

David's death reminded Barack of his mixed heritage and of his earlier quest to make a difference in the world. He soon quit his job and searched again for a meaningful position. He took a few temporary assignments at first—encouraging recycling, passing out flyers for a political race. After six months, he was broke and hungry, wondering where his downward spiral would end.

And then he got a call from Chicago.

Barack enjoyed a rare visit from his grandparents while studying at Columbia University.

chapter **5**

Community Organizer

Barack had been to Chicago once before. As a 10-year-old boy, he had visited the city with his mother, his grandmother, and Maya. The highlight had been seeing the shrunken heads of a man and woman on exhibit at the Field Museum. The heads were old. They could have belonged to anyone. The younger Barack was curious: Did the owners' descendants ever pass the display and unwittingly come face to face with a distance relative? It was impossible to know, but he liked thinking about it.

Now, however, Barack would be moving to Chicago on a permanent basis. The phone call he had received

Harold Washington (1922–1987)

Harold Washington grew up in Chicago, attending a segregated high school before dropping out. Following his service in World War II, he went to college and law school, then entered Illinois politics. He rose through the ranks as an advocate of civil rights issues. In 1983 he was elected mayor of Chicago, thanks to strong support in the black community and a split in the white vote between current mayor Jane Byrne and Richard M. Daley, the son of a former mayor.

Harold Washington (center) took the oath of office as Chicago's 42nd mayor on April 29, 1983.

was a job offer—one that was too good to refuse.

At the time of Barack's arrival in Chicago, the city had recently elected its first black mayor, Harold Washington. It was a somewhat surprising event for a city where the effects of segregation were still evident. Black people who had moved from the South to Chicago following the Civil War had been steered into ghettos and public housing, and forced into restrictive covenants. The result was lasting racial tension—and lasting disadvantages for the African-Americans who found themselves still stuck in those ghettos.

Barack's job was with the Developing Communities Project, a church-based community organization. His boss was a white

COVENANT

Covenants are agreements that, when used in real estate documents, can allow or prohibit certain actions on the part of a homeowner or renter.

organizer who had hired him for a practical reason—he needed a black man to work directly with the black community. Barack would assist

GRIEVANCES

Grievances are wrongs or injustices that often form the basis for a complaint against a higher authority.

laid-off workers on Chicago's South Side, trying to help them find new jobs. He would also search for general grievances to air. These might be neighborhood or housing-development issues, anything that the local government could fix if the problems were brought to its attention.

Barack started by introducing himself at local community meetings, interviewing anyone who was willing to speak to him. At first, nobody trusted him. He was an outsider, after all, not one of their own. But his boss was quick to give him some advice: If Barack wanted to make a connection with these people, he had to look below the surface. He needed to find out the "stuff that makes them tick."

Gradually, after months of hard work, Barack came to be accepted. People were willing to discuss their opinions about "a do-nothing alderman or the neighbor who refused to mow his lawn." The more experience he got, the more he learned about the backgrounds of the community members. Many of them were from other parts of Chicago—but wherever they were from, they were used to oppression. It no longer surprised them. But the relentlessness of it, the feeling that change would never come, had clearly worn them down.

Barack saw the limitations that activism sometimes presented. In the face of widespread layoffs, creating a job bank could help skilled workers replace jobs they had lost, but it wouldn't give high-school dropouts or

"Prison records had been passed down from father to son ..."
–Barack Obama, about Altgeld Gardens

unskilled workers the tools they needed to join the work force for the first time.

His early work focused on a public housing project called Altgeld Gardens. Altgeld's residents were so used to the disappointments of daily life that they had lost even the strength for outrage. There were gangs, drug dealers, shootings, sirens—chaos and danger at every turn. As Barack observed, "In places like Altgeld, prison records had been passed down from father to son for more than a generation."

He had some success over the next three years. For example, he prodded the city to clean up hazardous waste in some apartment complexes. More significantly, he was coming to realize that complicated issues couldn't be solved simply by untangling some political red tape or putting pressure on a lazy city agency.

In local high schools, many students were

Barack worked hard in Chicago trying to establish a trusting relationship with the members of the local community.

dropping out, giving up on life before they had even started, or turning to crime to make ends meet. A school counselor summed up the challenge: The critical point, he said, was to recognize that students were eager to learn when they could see the promise of becoming an important part of the world around them. "But for the black child, everything's turned upside down. From day one, what's he learning about? Someone else's history. Someone else's culture. Not only that, this culture he's supposed to learn from is the same culture that's systematically rejected him, denied his humanity."

How did people face such overwhelming barriers without getting crushed? Many of who attended the various nearby churches drew great strength from their religion. Barack envied

them. He was the first to admit that he had no such anchor. He had inherited a patchwork quilt of religion. His father had been raised a Muslim, his mother a Christian. But neither one had been religious as an adult. He remembered his mother's tales of hypocritical church ladies who judged others while hiding their own family secrets, and seemingly pious men who were devout on Sundays but cheated employees and promoted racism the rest of the week.

His mother's decision to remain apart from churches had suited her particular sense of independence. But in Chicago, Barack saw how a strong church created a supportive network of

Altgeld Gardens public housing development was a focus for much of Barack's work as a community organizer in Chicago.

The Trinity United Church of Christ in Chicago was the first church in which Barack Obama was an active member.

community. He missed that sense of belonging. Independence was important; it could also be lonely.

And so he was both delighted and overwhelmed to discover a church where he felt at home. The revelation surprised him. It happened when he heard a sermon preached by the Reverend Jeremiah Wright, Jr., a minister at the Trinity United Church of Christ. The sermon was called "The Audacity to Hope," and it brought Barack to tears. Hope was not about logic or practicality. Hope was an ideal, fed by faith. It could be beaten down, it could be delayed, but it could never be entirely erased. Barack decided he had found the church for him.

AUDACITY

Audacity is the boldness to act without regard for normal restraints.

Such thoughts also gave him the encouragement and reassurance he needed to take the next step forward. A community organizer could only do so much. Barack wanted to do more. Law school seemed like the logical next step. He believed that knowledge of the law could help him bring about real change. He wanted to learn about finance and currency, law-making, business, real estate, and banks. After his experience in Chicago, he felt ready to learn all of this—and to bring it back to Chicago and put it to work.

A few months later, he was accepted to Harvard Law School in Cambridge, Massachusetts, one of the most prestigious law schools in the country. Of course, Barack realized that there was a danger in taking this road to advancement. He would be tempted to leave the fighting to others. Why not be satisfied with being a good example, a shiny role model? He could work in the right firm, live in the right neighborhood, and make the right donations to the right causes.

But he had faith that he would find a different path. With luck, the audacity of hope would be his guide.

Obama gained spiritual strength from attending his church's services.

chapter **6**

Kenya

S ix years had passed since Barack's father's death. It was the summer of 1988, and he would be starting law school in the fall. But first, he was taking a long-delayed trip into his past. He was going to Kenya.

Barack admitted to himself that he was a little nervous about making the trip. It probably helped that he spent a few weeks traveling through Europe first. But then the moment arrived. In his mind, Africa had become more of a dream than an actual destination, "a new promised land, full of ancient traditions and sweeping vistas, noble struggles and talking drums." What if somehow the

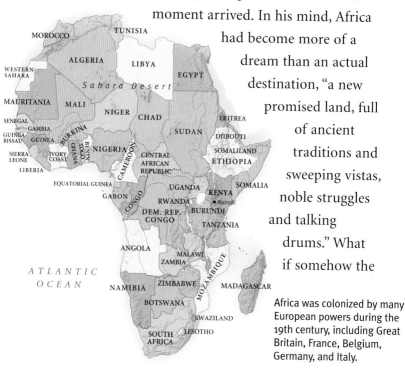

Africa was colonized by many European powers during the 19th century, including Great Britain, France, Belgium, Germany, and Italy.

reality of being there in person didn't measure up? What if he found himself disappointed with the place itself? He was anxious that a failure to connect with the place would reflect on more than just the place: It had to do with Barack Sr.'s leaving Hawaii, his death, and the ties that bound father and son—and son and heritage—together.

Modern Nairobi is a blend of traditional Kenyan and contemporary architecture.

Kenya was very much a country that reflected African history. First settled around 4,000 years ago, it had been home to many different tribes. The passing centuries saw the rise of farming, herding, and fishing. Later, Arab and Portuguese traders often visited the eastern coast. When Africa was colonized by European powers in the late 19th century, the country eventually ended up in British hands. After periods of strife in the 20th century, Kenya finally gained its independence in 1963.

COLONY

A colony is linked to a parent country politically, but is geographically separate.

When Barack arrived in the capital, Nairobi, he found himself staring at pieces of

Kenyan Independence

Kenyan independence did not bring with it an entirely peaceful transition. The first prime minister and later president, Jomo Kenyatta (circa 1894–1978), was thought to favor members of his own tribe in running the government. Tribal rivalries often got in the way of progress, a fact that Barack Obama, Sr., had clearly foreseen.

history everywhere he looked. The old British colonial influence was still evident in clothing styles and the sound of British accents, but it was intermingled with modern high-rise office buildings and elegant hotels. The pattern of old and new showed up everywhere: Women in tribal dress walked by slick, modern stores filled with luxury goods; businessmen in formal suits stopped to worship at a rustic mosque.

Barack's guide was his half sister, Auma, whom he had met in Chicago when she visited there. She had returned home to Kenya for an extended stay after doing graduate work in Germany. It was Auma who had given Barack a more complete picture of their father. The Old Man, as she called him, had experienced a dramatic rise and fall in the Kenyan government. He was smart and dedicated, but refused to play the political games necessary to stay in power. His abrupt honesty also rubbed many people the wrong way. When tensions rose among political factions, Auma told her brother, "the Old Man's friends just kept quiet and learned to live with the situation. But the Old

TRIBALISM

Tribalism is strong loyalty to a unified group or tribe.

Man began to speak up. He would tell the people that tribalism was going to ruin the country and that unqualified men were taking the best jobs. His friends tried to warn him about saying such things in public, but he didn't care."

These stories presented a different image of his father than the one his mother had described for him. It took some getting used to. And now that Barack was in Kenya itself, his feelings were harder to control. He had such a big and extended family. He met Auma's mother, Kezia (his father's first wife), and Kezia's sister, Jane (whom he had spoken

Barack poses with members of the Obama family during his visit to Kenya.

> *"My family seemed to be everywhere . . . all of them fussing and fretting over Obama's long-lost son."*
>
> –Barack Obama, of his extensive family in Kenya

to on the phone at the time of his father's death). He also got to know his half brothers, Abo, Roy, and Bernard. And beyond them was a host of cousins and other relatives spanning several generations. "My family seemed to be everywhere: in stores, at the post office, on streets or in the parks, all of them fussing and fretting over Obama's long-lost son."

Unfortunately, this large family did not have much extra money. Barack's father had been their main source of support, and he was sorely missed. Barack's Aunt Zeituni told him, when speaking of his father: "I am telling you, his problem was that his heart was too big. When he lived, he would just give to everyone who asked him. And they all asked."

As Barack took in the details around him, he noticed something familiar about them. In Aunt Jane's apartment, he observed "the

Barack visits with his step-grandmother, Sarah Obama.

The Great Rift Valley provided a dramatic backdrop to Barack's visit to the Kenyan countryside.

well-worn furniture, the two-year-old calendar, the fading photographs, the blue ceramic cherubs that sat on linen doilies." It reminded him of the apartments he'd seen in Altgeld—and of the people he had seen in them. Most notably, it seemed they were all women: mothers, daughters, children, talking, working, playing, and watching TV.

Everywhere he went during his journey, there was something new for Barack to absorb, to process. Coming to Kenya hadn't provided the tidy explanations he had been looking for. In fact, he had found even more variety—and more conflict—among the many parts that made up his history and heritage.

Still, Africa offered plenty to enjoy and appreciate, and Barack would fondly remember the details of his trip. His travels took him out into the countryside, where the landscape was dazzling. In the Great Rift Valley, he saw grasslands that seemed to stretch out forever. The landscape amazed him—clear views to the horizon, where the open savannah met the sky. In other places the land teemed with wildlife—herds of zebras and gazelles, lions, elephants, and wildebeests. The rivers revealed pink-eyed hippos peeking out from the water. Not every

Giraffes are at home in Kenya and in many other parts of Africa.

Sunrise near Mount Kilimanjaro in Kenya reveals a panoramic look at the African landscape.

scene was fit for a postcard, though. He also saw bloodied hyenas eating wildebeests while vultures watched patiently from the treetops, waiting for their turn to dine.

As Barack learned more about his family's history, he realized that what seemed like the distant past in America was much more immediate in Kenya. Europeans had only come to Kenya one hundred years earlier. Before that, children were educated at home by their parents, learning from their mothers to tend crops, build homes, and cook for their families, and from their fathers to herd animals, and wield traditional weapons like pangas and spears.

One story about Barack's own grandfather sounded like something out of a folk tale. Once upon a time, a man wanted to pass through Grandfather's land. But Grandfather refused

This is the home of Barack's step-grandmother, Sarah Obama, in Kogelo, Western Kenya.

to give permission because he thought the man's goat would eat some of his plants. The man protested. He insisted that his goat was very well behaved and would eat nothing. So Grandfather changed his mind—but with one condition: If the goat nibbled at even the smallest leaf, Grandfather would cut off its head. The man agreed to this. Surely, he thought, his goat would behave itself for just a few minutes. So Grandfather let them pass.

The goat had not gone more than a few feet when it reached out and bit off part of a leaf. A moment later—whoosh!—Grandfather brought his machete down and cut off the goat's head.

The man who owned the goat was very upset. How could Grandfather do such a thing over a small piece of leaf? Grandfather was calm and confident in his reply: "If I say I will do something, I will do it. Otherwise how will people know that my word is true?"

> *"If I say I will do something, I will do it."*
>
> – Hussein Ouyango Obama, Barack's Kenyan grandfather

Stories like these revealed much about Kenya. Values, at least on the surface, may differ from one place to another. But underneath, the universal truths remain. And there was no denying the strong connection Barack felt to this place and its people. His people. He felt a sense of responsibility toward them. How could he act on this? Community organizing wouldn't help his relatives—like Bernard, who struggled to find a job, or Jane, who could barely afford basic necessities.

For now, though, it was challenge enough to rip apart the fabric of his old life and try to weave in all these new strands. "I realized that who I was, what I cared about, was no longer just a matter of intellect or obligation, no longer a construct of words. I saw that my life in America—the black life, the white life, the sense of abandonment I'd felt as a boy, the frustration and hope I'd witnessed in Chicago—all of it was connected with this small plot of land an ocean away, connected by more than the accident of a name or the color of my skin."

He returned home to America with a lot to think about.

chapter **7**

Law School and Beyond

By the time Barack Obama started law school in the fall of 1988, he was 27, older than most of his fellow classmates. He was not the only first-year student that age, and he was not the only black student either. And no doubt somebody else had been raised in Hawaii or had spent a few years working for a nonprofit organization. But putting these traits all together, there was no one else there quite like him.

Harvard Law School was founded in 1817. Among its graduates through the years were President Rutherford B. Hayes and several Supreme Court justices, including Louis Brandeis and Oliver Wendell Holmes. There was also an assortment of governors, legal

For law student Barack Obama, Harvard University quickly felt like home.

scholars, and founders of successful law firms.

Barack did not imagine himself joining their ranks. He fully intended to work hard, but his classmates, he realized, were planning to work pretty hard, too. He had no particular expectations of making a name for himself. He joined the Black Law Students Association and wrote articles for some of the school law journals. But mostly he spent his spare time each day studying in the library.

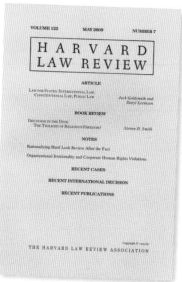

The *Harvard Law Review* has influence extending far beyond the borders of the law school campus.

Still, he managed to stand out. His grades and his professors' recommendations were excellent. At the end of his first year, he won a spot among the 80 law-review editors. These editors were all law students at Harvard. Collectively, they supervised the *Harvard Law Review,* a journal published monthly from November through June. Its articles were written by legal scholars from all over the country. The editors were not paid for their efforts, but the experience and prestige of participating often helped them win highly competitive jobs after graduation.

That summer Barack returned to Chicago to work as an intern for Sidley & Austin, a law firm that did a lot

of corporate business. Corporate law was not a strong interest of Barack's—it was a long way from community organizing—but the position paid well, and he needed the money to make a dent in his student loans.

Every intern was supervised by someone in the firm. Barack found himself assigned to a tall young lawyer named Michelle Robinson. Three years younger than Barack, she had already graduated from Harvard Law School herself, having enrolled right after graduating from Princeton.

Unlike Barack, Michelle had been born and raised in Chicago. Her father, Fraser, had worked for the city and her mother, Marian, had stayed home raising their two children before becoming a secretary at a local bank. For 20 years, Fraser had suffered from multiple sclerosis, but he had kept his sense of humor even as it became increasingly hard for him to get around.

Michelle had heard a lot about Barack even before they met. Other lawyers in the office had plenty of nice things to say about his looks, his intelligence, and his writing

> *"The home that Fraser and Marian Robinson had built . . . stirred a longing for stability and a sense of place."*
>
> –Barack Obama, writing about Michelle's family

ability. But she wasn't intrigued. A specialist in entertainment law, Michelle was intent on putting all her energy into her career.

Barack felt differently. Michelle was a fine supervisor, but from the moment they met, he hoped for more than a professional relationship. It took Michelle a little longer to return the feeling. At first, she didn't think it would be right for them to see each other socially. After all, she was supposed to be his advisor. Barack just laughed at her objections. He asked her out again and again, completely convinced that the firm would survive the encounter.

Finally, she agreed. On their first date, he took her out for ice

Barack considered himself a very lucky man to be dating Michelle Robinson.

Barack poses among his colleagues at the *Harvard Law Review*.

cream. They seemed to be getting along just fine, and at one point Barack asked if he could kiss her. With her permission, he did. The kiss, he remembered later, "tasted of chocolate."

As appealing as Michelle was on her own, Barack was drawn to her family as well. As he later wrote, being around the Robinsons and the home they had made together made him realize something he'd been looking for: a sense of place, of stability, of roots and home.

By the time he returned to Harvard in the fall, he and Michelle had become a couple. They maintained a long-distance relationship filled with late-night phone conversations. When Michelle's father died suddenly of complications after a kidney operation, Barack returned to her side to support her.

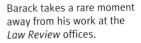

Back at school, he dedicated himself again to his studies, poring over statutes and cases. Barack found that studying law could be frustrating. At times, it seemed that its strict rules and outdated procedures didn't fit with the real world. And legal rules were often organized in ways that kept the powerful in power and explained to the powerless why their position should be accepted.

Nevertheless, the law intrigued him. And he soon found himself feeling ambitious enough to run for president of the *Law Review*. The president had final approval over the articles and notes published in each issue. It was a demanding, unpaid job, requiring as many as 60 hours a week (above and beyond the student's regular coursework). Naturally, the competition was intense for this prestigious position. However, being a few years older than the other students gave Barack an air of maturity, and his years as a community organizer had made him a good listener.

Barack takes a rare moment away from his work at the *Law Review* offices.

The *Law Review* editors deliberated for 17 hours before making their decision. Finally, they picked Barack. Some said afterward that he won because of the sense of fairness he projected. Even when he disagreed with people, he respected their right to have a different opinion.

As the first-ever black president of the *Harvard Law Review,* Barack attracted national attention. Articles about him appeared in major newspapers and national magazines. Job offers began to pour in. When he graduated in the spring of 1991, he probably could have gotten any position he wanted, even a clerkship on the United States Supreme Court.

But Barack did not pursue any of these opportunities. Remaining true to his earlier convictions, he returned to Chicago to practice civil rights law at the firm of Davis, Miner, Barnhill & Galland. In his law-school studies and his work on the *Law Review,* Barack challenged himself to find ways that the law could support common people, instead of just maintaining the status quo. If the system was too strong, too intimidating for the average person to take on, he would be there to help. In one case, for example, he worked successfully with his legal team to show how the state had ignored a law designed to make it easier for poor people to register to vote.

Most of the legal work he did focused on the inner-city community, and the people and businesses who lived and worked there: community groups, small business owners, churches, health clinics, grocers, and

STATUS QUO

The status quo is the current state of things.

The Clinton White House

The election of Bill Clinton (b. 1946) to the presidency in 1992 marked a return of the Democrats to the White House after 12 years of Republican leadership. President Clinton had wide support in the black community, and he was expected to make many improvements in the lives of poor and working-class people. However, a bumpy relationship with Congress and controversies in his personal life hampered him in these efforts.

community doctors. It was rewarding work, but it brought to light some ugly truths. From time to time, clients would come into his office and describe acts of discrimination and unfair treatment that hardly seemed possible in the modern world. Again and again, Barack saw and heard proof that much more work was needed before such injustices were laid to rest.

In 1992, Barack also began teaching constitutional law at the University of Chicago Law School. He wasn't interested in a career as a college professor, but he enjoyed the give-and-take with the students. He liked challenging their assumptions and listening to them challenge his in return. He found a strong appeal in the law-school classroom: "the stripped-down nature of it, the high-wire act of standing in front of a room at the beginning of each class with just blackboard and chalk."

Michelle and Barack look proud and happy in one their wedding portraits.

His personal life underwent some significant changes, too. On October 18, 1992, Barack and Michelle were married. The wedding was attended by many family members on both sides. Barack had also begun writing a book about himself, a book that became a memoir of his life. It traced the inner and outer journeys he had traveled on the way to discovering his identity. When *Dreams from My Father* was published in 1995, it received a lot of positive attention. The book was particularly applauded for the honesty with which its author had revealed the circumstances of his life.

Unfortunately, the celebration over the book did not last. Barack's mother, Ann, had been suffering from cancer, and had moved back from Asia to live with his grandmother in Hawaii. (His grandfather Stanley had passed away in 1992.) Ann died that November, and her death saddened Barack deeply. He knew that many of his best attributes—"honesty, empathy, discipline, delayed gratification and hard work"—had come from his mother. But he took some consolation knowing that she had spent her final years in a way that made her happy:

She had traveled the world and found ways to help people—whether helping women finance an education or procuring a sewing machine for a family in need. She spent time with friends, enjoyed the outdoors, and immersed herself in the cultures she encountered abroad. She treated herself to the small treasures that made her smile. She wrote, read, and communicated with her family.

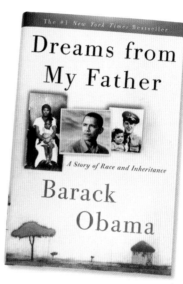

The cover of Barack's memoir features a few pictures from his family history.

Confident in her own sense of self, Ann had never tried to take the place of Barack's absent father. And she never criticized Barack Sr.'s failings. If anything, she was more forgiving of his behavior than she might have been. But this was not so surprising, for Barack understood that "she had an unswerving instinct for kindness, charity, and love, and spent much of her life acting on that instinct, sometimes to her detriment."

As he continued on his path through life, Barack would do his best to uphold the values she prized most.

> *"She had an unswerving instinct for kindness, charity, and love."*
>
> –Barack Obama, remembering his mother

chapter **8**

Politics Beckons

Barack Obama was living the American dream. He had graduated from both Columbia University and Harvard Law School with honors. He was a happily married newlywed living in a city he enjoyed and doing a job that brought him satisfaction. He had written a well-received book about his unusual upbringing. He was respected and liked by his peers, and he could still get up and down the basketball court with players half his age.

Still, the 34-year-old lawyer was restless. Something was missing. He was glad to be able to help his clients. But what about those people who never made it to his door? He wanted to be able to prompt change on a broader scale. As a community organizer, he had gone to lawmakers looking for support. As a lawyer, he had found ways to use existing laws to help people. He later wrote that the law was sometimes the only way to confirm and

State vs. Federal

Every state except Nebraska has both a house and a senate representing the citizens of its cities and districts. The districts in the house are smaller, which gives the citizens greater representation. This mirrors the structure of the United States Congress, which has both a larger House of Representatives (with 435 members representing the states) and a smaller Senate of 100 members (two for each state).

defend our values, "particularly when the rights and opportunities of the powerless in our society are at stake."

But he couldn't make or change laws on his own. And even helping clients with individual problems didn't offer a larger sense of progress. Three years earlier, Barack had gotten a taste of what could be accomplished when he directed Illinois Project Vote, an organization that worked to register 100,000 new minority voters. That experience, he recognized, touched many lives at once.

Obama's first political goal was to become a state senator working at the Illinois state capitol in Springfield.

Maybe this was the time to put all his experience together. If he wanted to influence society at large, politics was the place to be. Barack was inspired by the American political tradition, from its roots with the founding fathers through the momentous changes of the civil rights movement, "a tradition based on the simple idea that we have a stake in one another, and that what binds us together is greater than what drives us apart."

As it happened, a state senator from Illinois's 13th district, Alice Palmer, was planning to run for the U.S. House of

Representatives, vacating her seat in the state senate. Her old district covered some of Chicago's South Side, an area Barack knew well. Seeing his chance, he decided to run for her seat. However, there was nothing automatic about his chances for victory. Growing up in Hawaii might look intriguing on a law-school application, but it wasn't a plus in the rough-and-tumble world of Illinois politics. He hadn't come up from the streets. And while he had lived in Chicago for a number of years, he didn't have an extended family or political network to lean on for support. And as a practical matter in racial politics, there was also the question of his skin color. Nobody would question Barack's calling himself black. But he was

Obama worked tirelessly in his first campaign to meet the voters in his district.

Much of the business of governing Illinois takes place on the floor of the senate inside the Illinois state capitol.

light-skinned, and therefore potentially "not black enough" to satisfy some people in the predominantly African-American districts.

None of these hurdles stopped him. As he later wrote, "I talked to anyone who would listen. I went to block club meetings and church socials, beauty shops and barber shops. If two guys were standing on a corner, I would cross the street to hand them campaign literature." And everywhere he went, he was asked the same two questions: Where did he get his funny name, and why would a nice guy like him want to get into politics?

Answering those questions wasn't so hard. He was named after his father, of course, and as for politics, he had a true desire to serve. He brought his energy, his sense of conviction to the voters—and they liked what they saw. He won the Democratic primary and then the general election.

Senator Obama was excited to work in the capitol at Springfield. However, the newly minted state legislator was only one of many. Nobody was putting him in charge of anything, or even paying much attention to his presence.

Republicans controlled the state legislature, and freshmen Democrats like Obama were almost invisible.

INTERROGATION

An interrogation is an interview, usually done in a police station, in which suspects are questioned about their possible involvement in a crime.

Still, he got involved. A particular issue that he had success with was campaigning for death-penalty reforms. One big criticism of the death penalty is that there's no turning back afterward, no chance to correct an injustice once the execution has taken place. Yet sometimes new evidence surfaces months or even years later. To reduce one potential area for mistakes, Obama backed legislation that required the police to videotape any questionings of suspects in major crimes. With all the interrogations recorded, there would be no chance of misinterpreting what was said.

Obama gained valuable experience at the state level, but at the end of his second two-year term, he decided to run for the U.S. House of Representatives. He knew that if his bid was successful, he could have

Obama often spoke up on the floor of the state senate about the issues that concerned him.

Malia, shown here during her father's primary concession speech on March 21, 2000. experienced an early introduction to politics.

an impact nationally, far beyond what was possible in Springfield. The congressman currently in the job was Representative Bobby Rush. Unlike Obama's first stab at politics, the attempt would not involve running for an open seat. Representative Rush had every intention of holding onto his job. Obama went ahead with his campaign anyway.

The campaign did not go well. Aside from having a hard time convincing voters that they should unseat an incumbent, he was hampered by various events beyond his control. "It was an ill-considered race," he wrote later, "and I lost badly—the sort of drubbing that awakens you to the fact that life is not obliged to work out as you'd planned."

So Obama returned to the state senate. Happily, life was not only about politics. Important changes at home were drawing more and more of his attention, and in a very good way. The Obamas' first daughter, Malia, was born in 1998, and her sister, Natasha (called Sasha), followed in 2001. Barack delighted in his daughters and the time he spent with them.

INCUMBENT

An incumbent is the holder of a political office, and during an election has the advantage of already being in the position that his or her opponents want.

The young Obama family spent time together whenever possible.

However, he was also aware that a political life, with its long evening dinners, unexpected travel delays, and last-minute meetings, was not the best match for a rich family life.

Obama was continuing to make a name for himself in the state senate, but he made a bigger impression one day at an antiwar rally in Chicago in 2002. At the time, many people disagreed with the idea of a U.S. invasion of Iraq, a step that seemed likely in the near future. They had gathered that fall day to voice their anger and disapproval. Obama was scheduled to speak, but he wasn't sure the crowd would want to hear everything he had to say. As he later told a reporter, "I noticed that a lot of people at that rally were wearing buttons saying, 'War Is Not an Option.' And I thought, I don't agree with that. Sometimes war is an option. The Civil War was worth fighting. World War II. So I got up and said that." He also said, most notably, "I am not opposed to all wars. I'm opposed to dumb wars." Invading and occupying Iraq would be "a rash war, a war based not on reason but on passion, not on principle but on politics."

Despite the attention he gained, Obama could not shake the feeling that his career in politics was becoming permanently stalled. And if that was the case, perhaps he should move on. He had done his civic duty. Perhaps it was time to turn his attention elsewhere.

But before making that decision, he considered taking one last chance to move up or out, "to try out my ideas before I settled into a calmer, more stable, and better-paying existence." An open seat for the U.S. Senate was shaping up in Illinois for 2004. Obama would be an underdog in the contest. Indeed, he would be one of several underdogs in a crowded field. But he remained hopeful. Michelle, who enjoyed a more orderly, predictable life for her family, was somewhat reluctant. However, she agreed to support him in giving politics one more shot.

> ## The Iraq War
>
> The war in Iraq started in March 2003. President George W. Bush justified the attack by explaining that the Iraqi government under President Saddam Hussein possessed weapons of mass destruction that posed a direct threat to American security. At first, the war was popular with the American public. However, the conflict ended up lasting much longer than expected. This, combined with the fact that no weapons of mass destruction were ever found, caused support for the war to decline sharply during Bush's second term.

"I am not opposed to all wars. I'm opposed to dumb wars."

–Barack Obama, in a 2002 speech

9

Run for the Senate

The race for the 2004 Democratic nomination for the United States Senate in Illinois was not for the faint of heart. There were seven primary candidates

> **PRIMARY**
>
> In a primary (preliminary) election, a single political party elects a candidate to represent that party in a general (main) election.

in all. Several of them were popular, well connected, and supported by ample funds.

And then there was Barack Obama. While not a complete unknown, he had neither significant financial support nor a well-oiled statewide organization. But he ignored these shortcomings. In this campaign, he would share his ideas, his vision of America. There would be no second-guessing, no looking over his shoulder.

Some people dismissed him as corny or sentimental. Obama, they said, was ignoring the hard-nosed realities of the

> **The Senate Seat**
>
> The U.S. Senate seat that Obama was running for had been held by Peter Fitzgerald, who left it to to retire. Six years earlier, Carol Moseley Braun had represented Illinois in the Senate, the first woman and the first African-American to do so. In 2004, she decided to run for president (unsuccessfully, in the end). Had she chosen instead to run again for her old Senate seat, Obama would not have run against her.

times. He didn't agree. He thought voters were sick and tired of the same old mudslinging. In his mind, he could lose the election, but he could not fail as long as he got the chance to speak out.

As Obama was quick to point out, "it sometimes appears that Americans today value nothing so much as being rich, thin, young, famous, safe and entertained."

Obama found running for the U.S. Senate, a statewide office, much more daunting than his earlier, local campaigns.

This was not the America that he believed in—and not one that many Americans would admit to. But that didn't mean there wasn't truth in his words. Making America realize its potential demanded more than vague support or an empty promise. He later wrote, "If we aren't willing to pay a price for our values, if we aren't willing to make some sacrifices in order to realize them, then we should ask ourselves whether we truly believe in them at all."

His campaign stops took him to every corner of Chicago and up and down the state of Illinois, past farms and small towns, along six-lane highways and winding dirt roads.

In 2004, most Illinois democrats supported Obama in the state election and John Kerry for president.

As Obama listened to people, to their concerns and aspirations, he paid close attention. He took note of how many beliefs people seemed to have in common. Time after time, he heard that people should be able to find jobs with fair wages, healthcare that didn't break the bank, and quality education for their children. Obama tried to show voters that he understood their concerns: "They wanted to be safe, from criminals and from terrorists; they wanted clean air, clean water, and time with their kids. And when they got old, they wanted to be able to retire with some dignity and respect."

Obama's eloquence was not enough to make him a frontrunner at first. One of his opponents, a wealthy businessman named Blair Hull, was pulling ahead under an avalanche of paid promotion. Hull spent millions and millions of dollars on his campaign. He might well have won the election, except for one thing: In the final weeks, negative news about his personal life became public and doomed his chances.

> *"They believed that every child should have a genuinely good education."*
>
> – Barack Obama, summarizing the common themes among citizens

Obama's campaign surged in those same weeks. Earlier support from several key unions was bolstered by endorsements from important newspapers

UNION

A union is a group of workers in a common type of job who band together to negotiate better working conditions for themselves.

around the state, including the Chicago newspapers, the *Tribune* and the *Sun-Times*. When the primary results were counted, Obama had won with an impressive 53 percent of the vote. This was remarkable considering that the vote had been split seven ways. He had also won a number of the Chicago suburbs, communities that political experts did not think would support a black candidate for statewide office.

Some people thought Obama had gotten lucky in the primary—and maybe he had. But still, people had liked what he had to say enough to pick his name in the voting booth. One of the people clearly impressed was Senator John Kerry of Massachusetts. Kerry had emerged as the victor in the Democratic presidential primaries. In July, he was going to be named as the Democratic candidate for president. The Democratic National Convention, the party meeting where nominees were officially selected, would

be held in Boston. As usual, there were would be speeches and more speeches. But one of them, the keynote speech, was considered very important.

ENDORSEMENT

An endorsement is a formal announcement by an individual or organization to publicly show support for a specific political candidate.

Obama catapulted himself onto the national stage with his rousing and thoughtful speech at the 2004 Democratic Convention.

It often served as a springboard for a younger politician, a chance to be seen on the national stage.

And Kerry chose Barack Obama to give this critical speech.

So on a Tuesday night, in front of thousands of people at the convention itself, and with millions more watching on television, Barack Obama gave the best speech of his life.

He began by reaffirming that what made America great was not its wealth or power, but its belief in the values embedded in the Declaration of Independence.

Touching on one of his recurring themes, Obama spoke about what Americans valued most: "a faith in simple dreams, an insistence on small miracles; that we can tuck in our children at night and know that they are fed and clothed and safe from harm; that we can say what we think, write what we think, without hearing a sudden knock on the door; that we can have an idea and start our own business without paying a bribe; that we can participate in the political process without fear of retribution."

People, he insisted, did not want government to do everything for them. But with a little help in the right places, Americans could face brighter prospects for their own futures and the futures of their children. To Obama, this was not a fanciful dream. It was an attainable goal.

Most of all, he saw the promise of "hope in the face of difficulty, hope in the face of uncertainty, the audacity of hope: In the end, that is God's greatest gift to us, the bedrock of this nation, a belief in things not seen, a belief that there are better days ahead."

There was more, and all of it was electrifying. In those few minutes, Barack Obama went from being a state politician known to his Illinois

Obama joined the Democratic presidential nominee, Senator John Kerry of Massachusetts, at the closing ceremonies of the 2004 convention.

Obama debates his Republican opponent, Alan Keyes, during his campaign for the U.S. Senate.

constituents to a major figure on the national stage. The speech also put increased scrutiny on the Illinois race for the senate in a new light, a race that had already shifted more than expected.

The original Republican nominee in the Illinois race, Jack Ryan, had been forced to drop out when personal problems surfaced concerning his former marriage. In his place, the Republicans had recruited Alan Keyes, a black political activist and a former ambassador to the United Nations.

It was the first time in American history that two black candidates had vied for a Senate seat. On paper, Keyes's background made him a worthy opponent. But detractors noted some important drawbacks, as well: He had never lived in Illinois, the state he wanted to represent; he had never won an election; and many people, even in his own party, found him tough to tolerate.

That fall, Alan Keyes challenged Obama's religion and his "blackness," among other things. For his part, Obama found Keyes to be "fierce and unyielding," and noted that even his political colleagues were intimidated by him. Keyes's personal manner was off-putting as well, since he "made no effort to conceal what he clearly considered to be his moral and intellectual superiority."

In the end, the Illinois election was not even close. On November 2, George W. Bush was re-elected to a second term as president, maintaining a Republican hold on the White House. But in Illinois, the Democratic candidate for the Senate won 70 percent of the vote.

Mr. Obama was going to Washington.

The Obama family enjoys the new senator's victory on election night— November 2, 2004— in a blizzard of confetti.

chapter **10**

Moving to Washington

The political mood in Washington, D.C., in January 2005 varied a great deal depending on who you asked. Republicans were pleased that President George W. Bush had won re-election despite the fact that the war in Iraq was not going as smoothly as planned. They had also retained control of both the House of Representatives and the Senate. So they would have at least another two more years, another election cycle, to be in charge.

Naturally, the Democrats held the opposite view. They were disappointed that John Kerry had lost the election. They were also frustrated that they had not done better in the congressional races. As they saw it, the Republicans were doing many things wrong. However, Democrats had been unable to convince the majority

The United States Capitol was Senator Obama's new workplace once he moved to Washington.

of the American people to agree with them.

One of the few Democratic bright spots was the election of the new junior senator from Illinois. Surrounded by family and friends, Barack Obama took the oath of office on January 4, 2005. It was a proud day for the extended Obama family, with representatives from Hawaii, Illinois, and Kenya attending. The new senator cherished the moment. He took the opportunity to show Malia and Sasha around the Capitol building, because they would not be visiting there often. He and Michelle had decided to keep their home in Chicago and not move the girls to Washington.

Malia and Sasha enjoyed visiting Washington and watching a re-enactment of their father's swearing-in ceremony on January 4, 2005.

African-Americans in the U.S. Senate

The first African-American elected to the U.S. Senate was Hiram Revels (1827–1901) of Mississippi. The former slave served from 1870 to 1871. Four years later, Blanche K. Bruce (1841–1898), also of Mississippi, became the first African American to serve a full six-year senate term. After that, laws discriminating against African-Americans kept them out of politics for decades. Finally, those laws were repealed in the 1960s, and in 1967, the third African-American U.S. senator was elected: Edward W. Brooke III from Massachusetts.

Obama was now the country's only African-American senator, and only the fifth ever to serve in that office, so naturally he drew a lot of attention from the press. At first, he tried to deflect some of this focus. When asked about beginning his Senate career, he struck a humble note. Out of the 100 senators, Obama commented, "I will be ranked 99th in seniority. I am going to be spending the first several months of my career in the U.S. Senate looking for the washroom and trying to figure out how the phones work."

But he was actually doing a lot more than that. He put together an experienced staff, people who had worked in Congress a long time. He got appointed to various committees, some of which, like the Foreign Relations committee, would enlarge his knowledge about America's place in the world. As one of the youngest senators, he was also among the most comfortable with new technologies. One of the early bills he developed allowed Americans to go online and see how tax dollars were spent.

The new senator was determined to avoid the impression of conducting politics as usual. He noted, "Most people who serve in Washington have been trained either as lawyers or as political operatives—professions that tend to place a premium on winning arguments rather than solving problems." He wanted to change the political climate if he could. Everyone was always so busy

COMMITTEE

A committee is a group of senators who meet to discuss issues concerning a single area of government.

sticking labels on their opponents and drawing ideological lines that could not be crossed. In such an atmosphere, it was almost impossible to make progress on any important issues.

Obama hoped to break down some of the rigid political walls that were keeping people apart. He wrote that "our democracy might work a bit better if we recognized that all of us possess values that are worthy of respect: if liberals at least acknowledge that the recreational hunter feels the same way about his gun as they feel about their library books, and if conservatives recognized that most women feel as protective of their right to reproductive freedom as evangelicals do of their right to worship."

It was refreshing to hear such sentiments voiced in public. But just saying them could not change the existing climate. And complicating Obama's ability to work for consensus behind the scenes was the fact that his days as a private person were gone. Easily recognizable, he was often cornered at social or political events. Over drinks and appetizers,

Obama met with his fellow senators in May 2005 to discuss the nomination of John Bolton as the U.S. ambassador to the United Nations.

Mr. SARBANES

many Democrats would complain to him about the various
actions of the Bush administration, expecting that he would
join in their chorus.

Obama was usually more measured in his response. First,
he insisted that "by nature I'm not somebody who gets real
worked up about things." Staying calm, he reasoned, was a
much more effective first step in beginning a negotiation
or resolving a dispute. Just as importantly, he was a student
of history. "When Democrats rush up to me at events
and insist that we live in the worst of political times, that
a creeping fascism is closing its grip around our throats,

Senator Obama often met
with the press to discuss
current concerns under the
Senate's jurisdiction.

> *"most people who serve in Washington have been trained . . . [in] winning arguments rather than solving problems."*
>
> – Barack Obama, *The Audacity of Hope*

I may mention the internment of Japanese Americans under FDR, the Alien and Sedition Acts under John Adams, or a hundred years of lynching under several dozen administrations as having been possibly worse, and suggest we all take a deep breath."

Such comments shocked many people. Obama did not give the easy answer, the political answer. He truly seemed to be speaking his mind. He was similarly open in discussing another popular target, the "special interests" that many people felt were really running the country. "I've never been entirely comfortable with the term "special interests," he wrote, "which lumps together ExxonMobil and bricklayers, the pharmaceutical lobby and the parents of special-ed kids." Indeed, the senator saw an important difference between corporate lobbyists (professionals paid by rich companies to promote a particular point of view) and groups of people with a cause in common, coming together to raise a common voice.

Obama's daily schedule as a senator was a full one. It was filled with meetings of every description. He wrote speeches, he gave speeches, and he listened to speeches. There were business breakfasts, political lunches, and fund-raising dinners. He looked over legislation, voted on the Senate floor, met with constituents, and posed for an endless series of pictures. If he wanted to catch his breath, he had to make an appointment.

However busy he was with work, Senator Obama often thought of his family. As someone who had grown up without a father in the house, he was determined that his daughters would not feel the same absence that he had. As part of his weekly schedule, he tried to get home to Illinois early enough on Thursdays to put the girls to bed. After spending Fridays working in Chicago, he would have the weekend to spend with his family. On Saturdays, he was not a senator—he was a dad and a husband, playing with his children or doing chores like laundry or grocery shopping. Then, on Sunday nights, he would leave again for Washington to begin another week.

When Senator Obama took office in January 2005, he had every intention of serving out his full term. He said so clearly on the day after he was elected. "I am not running for president," he stated at the time. "I am not running for president in four years. I am not running for president in 2008."

But over the next year and a half, he began to change his mind. By the fall of 2006, the 2008 presidential campaign was beginning to take shape. Senator Hillary Clinton of New York was the early frontrunner for the Democratic nomination. A senator since 2001, she was also the wife of former president

Bill Clinton and had served as first lady for the eight years of his presidency. Understandably, Senator Clinton was well known nationally, and she had already raised a lot of money for her campaign. Her support cut across a wide spectrum of Democrats and was particularly strong among women. There were other people, however, who were unhappy at the prospect of essentially handing her the nomination. It wasn't necessarily Senator Clinton's views that upset them. It was more the idea that the presidency was beginning to look like a private club with only two families as members. President George H.W. Bush, inaugurated in 1989, had been succeeded by President Bill Clinton in 1993. He in turn had

Senator Obama takes a moment to talk with his daughters before they head off to school from their home in Hyde Park, Chicago.

been followed by President George W. Bush (the son of the earlier president) in 2001. Was it really time again for another President Clinton in 2009?

Another factor was the strong encouragement Senator Obama received as he traveled around the country. The voters who were looking for change were drawn to him. He might not have the experience of other candidates, but he also didn't carry their political baggage. Partly, this was because he simply hadn't had the time to make too many unpopular votes. But he also didn't seem like a typical politician. Obama didn't try to please all of the people all of the time. He got people excited in a way that had not been seen for many years.

Shown here in his official Senate photograph, Senator Obama had a national profile, but was still considered new to the political scene.

There was also the idea of seizing the moment. The presidential election of 2008 would not involve an incumbent candidate—by law,

> *"Are you going to try to be president? Shouldn't you be vice president first?"*
>
> –Malia Obama, speaking to her father

President Bush could not seek a third term. That gave any new candidate a better chance than if he or she were running against a president already in office. If Obama waited four more years—or eight or twelve—things could be different. It was hard to predict who would be president at the time, or what new figure might have appeared on the political landscape. And meanwhile, the longer he was a senator, the less he would look like a breath of fresh air.

Running for president would be a bold move to say the least. And not everyone applauded the idea. Who did Obama think he was, wondered some critics? How arrogant was he to believe that two years in the Senate and a few more at the state level had prepared him for the most difficult job in the world? Even his daughter Malia asked him: "Are you going to try to be president? Shouldn't you be vice president first?"

Senator Obama was the first to admit he still had a lot to learn. And the critics might be right to protest. But he also had a vision of the kind of America he wanted to live in. And he was determined to help America get there.

chapter

11
Chasing the Nomination

February 10, 2007, was a bitterly cold day in Springfield, Illinois. Outside the Old State Capitol building, Senator Barack Obama stood before a large crowd to make an announcement. The chosen location was no accident. It was the same place that Abraham Lincoln had spoken in 1858 when he was launching his campaign for the senate.

In his speech, Obama described how the theme of hope appeared again and again the nation's history: in daring to challenge the abuses of the British Empire, in reforging the nation after the Civil War, through work projects during the Great Depression, and in offering new homes and new frontiers to immigrants and explorers alike.

He spoke of the challenges facing America today. These challenges were neither

Ignoring the cold, Senator Obama was bare-handed as he announced his candidacy for President of the United States.

simple nor small, and included the ongoing war in Iraq, dependence on foreign oil suppliers, failing schools, and unfair wages for honest work.

"What's stopped us from meeting these challenges," he said, "is not the absence of sound policies and sensible plans. What's stopped us is the failure of leadership, the smallness of our politics—the ease with which we're distracted by the petty and trivial, our chronic avoidance of tough decisions, our preference for scoring cheap political points instead of rolling up our sleeves and building a working consensus to tackle big problems."

Obama campaign buttons emphasized different aspects of the 2008 drive for the presidency.

He cited the example of Lincoln before him, a man who faced adversity time and again. "But through his will and his words, he moved a nation and helped free a people." It was also Lincoln, he added later, who "tells us that there is power in words. He tells us that there is power in conviction. That beneath all the differences of race and region, faith and station, we are one people."

Obama spoke well. His words reflected his deeply held convictions. But he was not as confident concerning the outcome of the campaign. Running for president was the biggest political risk he had ever taken. His chances of winning were unpredictable at best. Of course, he could always run

**Abraham Lincoln
(1809–1865)**

After losing in his first run for the White House, Abraham Lincoln was president during one of the most tumultuous periods in U.S. history: the Civil War. Determined to protect the Union, Lincoln—and his memorable speeches—would go down in history for opposing slavery and his passionate belief in the country he served.

again. But if he lost now, much of the luster that he carried as a new face on the national stage would be lost.

Throughout most of 2007, Senator Clinton seemed to be firmly in the lead. The remaining viable candidates included former Senator John Edwards of North Carolina, who had been John Kerry's running mate three years earlier; Governor Bill Richardson of New Mexico; and Senator Joe Biden of Delaware. All of these men were seasoned campaigners, though they lacked Senator Clinton's broad base of support.

In his speeches, Obama emphasized several issues. First, he had consistently opposed the war in Iraq. Further, he was committed to decreasing America's dependence on oil, lowering taxes on low-income workers, and providing universal health care.

The other candidates shared many of these views. What set Obama apart was an articulate presence, a youthful vigor,

The early frontrunner, Senator Hillary Clinton, is met by a large crowd at a campaign stop in Hammond, Indiana.

and an unabashed sincerity. Rare among political figures, he could rouse a convention hall of thousands and still seem like someone you could have dinner with afterward.

The passing weeks revealed that Obama was a tireless campaigner. He rose at dawn to greet factory workers starting their shift. Fourteen hours later, he could be found giving an after-dinner speech. Early on, he attracted many idealistic young supporters who were sent to work in key states. He also revolutionized the business of raising money over the Internet, taking in tens of millions of dollars in small contributions. The other candidates underestimated his appeal at first. By the time they realized their mistake, it was too late.

All of these strengths helped Senator Obama win a surprise victory in the Iowa caucuses in January 2008. A week later, Senator

Former Senator John Edwards, the 2004 vice presidential nominee, campaigned hard to win the 2008 nomination.

Counting Delegates

Delegates, or representative voters, are assigned in each state based on voting during the primary season. (There are also super delegates, officials from around the country who can support any candidate they wish.) At the national convention, the delegates' votes determine which candidate the party will support in the general election. Keeping track of how many delegates a candidate has can help him or her figure out where to put time, energy, and money as the campaign progresses—and at what point the candidacy is secure.

Clinton made her case by winning the first primary in New Hampshire. By this point, it was clear that the nomination would be a fight between Obama and Senator Clinton. In a primary election, each state holds a primary or caucus with a set number of delegates at stake, which the candidates usually win in proportion to the votes they receive in that state. (A few states have winner-take-all primaries, which increases the pressure in those places.)

For the next few months, the two candidates swapped victories in one primary after another. Each win brought with it a group of committed delegates, and both Obama and Clinton steadily increased their totals. But the momentum—and the lead—slowly turned Obama's way.

One major controversy Obama faced concerned the pastor of his church, the Reverend Jeremiah Wright, Jr. Reverend Wright made several speeches and television appearances concerning what he saw as the bitter racism in America. Obama was asked repeatedly if he shared Reverend Wright's views.

This was a painful situation. The senator and the reverend had been close since Obama's days as a community organizer, and the reverend had officiated at Barack and Michelle's wedding. However, Obama did not agree with him on all points, and hoped to leave it at that.

Unfortunately, Wright's comments became more and more outrageous. Finally, Obama renounced him, and resigned from his church. "The profound mistake of Reverend Wright's sermons," he said, "is not that he spoke about racism in our society. It's that he spoke as if our society was static, as if no progress has been made; as if this country—a country that has made it possible for one of his own members to run for the highest office in the land and build a coalition of white and black, Latino and Asian, rich and poor, young and old—is still irrevocably bound to a tragic past."

Senator Obama met with an enthusiastic crowd of supporters during a campaign rally in Austin, Texas.

A European Tour

In July 2008, Obama made a much-publicized trip to Europe. There he met with the leaders of several countries. In a major speech in Berlin, he extended some of his views on building bridges to the international arena. Some critics thought Obama was presumptuous to make such a trip when he was only a candidate and not the president himself. But Obama was willing to absorb such comments as a trade-off for the chance to appear presidential (and be treated presidentially by leaders of other countries) on the international stage.

Obama was making a significant point. Racism was not merely an issue in the past. At the same time, it was dishonest to inflame opinions by ignoring the progress that had been made.

In early June, Obama passed the 2,118-delegate mark. The nomination was his, regardless of how many votes Senator Clinton collected. A few days later, Clinton ended her campaign, throwing her support to him.

The Democratic National Convention was held in Denver that August. As the presidential nominee, Obama had the right to pick the party's vice presidential candidate. After much deliberation, he chose Senator Joe Biden of Delaware as his running mate. A former lawyer and county councilman, the 65-year-old Biden had been a senator since 1973. He was also considered an expert on foreign affairs, an area in which Senator Obama lacked experience.

The convention featured speeches by former president Bill Clinton, former vice president Al Gore,

RUNNING MATE

A running mate is one of two partners in a political party trying to be elected together as a team.

Michelle Obama, and her brother Craig Robinson, as well as a tribute to Senator Edward M. Kennedy—all designed to drum up enthusiasm for the main event.

On August 28, Barack Obama officially accepted his party's nomination. Breaking with tradition, he accepted the role not in the convention hall, but in an open-air stadium. More than 80,000 people heard him make his acceptance speech in person, and millions more watched on television to hear what the country's first black presidential nominee would say on this historic night.

The candidate laid out some hard truths: "Tonight, more Americans are out of work and more are working harder for less. More of you have lost your homes and even more are watching your home values plummet. More of you have cars you can't afford

The two running mates, Barack Obama and Joe Biden, wave to the crowd following Obama's acceptance speech.

to drive, credit card bills you can't afford to pay, and tuition that's beyond your reach."

It was not news to most people that the United States was at a difficult crossroads—it would become clearer during the course of the election just how difficult conditions were. What Americans needed to know before casting their votes was this: What could the president and the government do about it? According to Obama, Republicans had a habit of turning their backs on many Americans. If you had lost your job, lacked health care, or were born into poverty, the Republicans said, "Tough luck, you're on your own."

Obama, on the other hand, believed there were certain important jobs that the federal government could and

should do: "Protect us from harm and provide every child a decent education; keep our water clean and our toys safe; invest in new schools, and new roads, and science, and technology."

Obama finished his speech by invoking the memory of Martin Luther King, Jr., reminding his audience about the speech that King had given 45 years earlier in Washington, D.C. On that day, as King stood in front of the Lincoln Memorial, he could have fueled the rage and frustration of those in the crowd before him. Instead, he spoke of unity, of joining together, because "in America, our destiny is inextricably linked, that together our dreams can be one."

Senator Obama gives his acceptance speech to the Democratic National Convention and other supporters at Invesco Field in Denver, Colorado.

chapter **12**

The 2008 Election

While the Democrats were busy choosing their candidate for president, the Republicans were doing the same. But in 2008, Republicans were quicker to make up their minds. The Republicans settled on their nominee, Senator John McCain of Arizona, several months earlier than the Democrats picked Obama to run against him.

John McCain was born in 1936, the son and grandson of navy admirals. He graduated from the Naval Academy in 1958 and later became a navy aviator. In 1967, during the Vietnam War, he was captured when his plane was shot down. He spent the next five and a half years as a prisoner of war in North Vietnam. During this time, McCain earned his reputation as a hero, both for his courage as a prisoner and for refusing to accept an early release, a privilege offered to him

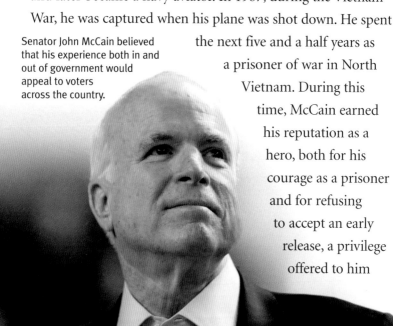

Senator John McCain believed that his experience both in and out of government would appeal to voters across the country.

because of his father's high rank. Sometimes tortured, and often placed in solitary confinement, he endured physical and mental abuse until he was freed in 1973.

Nine years later, in 1982, McCain successfully ran for the U.S. House of Representatives, moving up to the Senate in 1987. During the 1990s, he gained a reputation for being a maverick, for going his own way.

Following the Vietnam War, John McCain was welcomed home as a hero.

He emphasized this trait when making his first run for the presidency in 2000. However, in that year, he bowed out of the race after losing several key primaries to George W. Bush.

Now he was back. One of his biggest hurdles was overcoming the perception that his time had passed, that he should be content to sit on the sidelines. Even with the nomination in hand, he was still subject to questions about his age. Were the demands of the presidency too much for a man who would be 72 upon taking office?

Political observers expected McCain to pick a running mate from among the men who had run against him for the nomination. Or perhaps he would pick a friend who was a senator or governor from an important state where he needed support. Whatever his initial thoughts, in the end he surprised friends and foes alike by selecting Governor Sarah Palin of Alaska.

Governor Palin's image as an attractive mother of five with deeply held conservative views found supporters all over the country.

Born in Idaho in 1964, Sarah Heath moved with her family to Alaska as a baby. She married Todd Palin in 1988, and later entered politics as a city councilor, and then mayor, of Wasilla, Alaska. In 2006, she was elected governor of Alaska.

Governor Palin was almost unknown outside of her state. But under the white-hot glare of the media, she quickly invigorated the campaign.

As the campaigns picked up in September, both sides had to be careful in discussing the opposition. Obama had to be mindful of the fact that Senator McCain was a decorated war hero; Obama himself had never served in the military. So while he could criticize his opponent's views, Obama could never suggest that McCain lacked integrity or courage.

Senator McCain had to be careful as well. Win or lose, Senator Obama was already making history as the first African-American to win the nomination of a major party. Many voters, black and white, had never expected to see such an event in their lifetimes. If McCain were to criticize Obama in the wrong way, he could be accused of racism.

For the most part, both candidates were cautious. With the help of the Internet and the latest technology, Obama and his staff concentrated on raising money and getting out the vote. They built an army of volunteers in each state, all carefully organized and accounted for. The political energy and excitement that Obama sparked in his supporters had not been seen in decades.

Of course, Obama had weaknesses, too. It was widely recognized that his greatest vulnerability lay in foreign affairs. Having a father from Kenya and spending years living in Indonesia did not count as experience when dealing with complex international issues. And Senator McCain considered foreign affairs his strength. He was very comfortable in the world of missile systems and troop deployments. Given ongoing American concerns about terrorism, the needs of national security seemed to give McCain the advantage.

But then the economy fell. Actually, it had been falling since the spring, like a balloon that had sprung a slow leak. But in September, the balloon just popped. The stock market plunged, and huge companies, American institutions in the

The patriotic theme of the McCain-Palin campaign was "Country First."

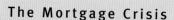

The Mortgage Crisis

One of the major causes of the economy's collapse in 2008 was the mortgage crisis. Weak regulations had allowed unsound loans to be offered to home buyers, and many people secured loans to buy homes that they would have trouble paying back. The combination of falling home prices and massive job losses led to an unprecedented number of people defaulting (failing to make payments) on their mortgage loans—which in turn made the situation even worse.

automotive and financial industries, were suddenly at risk of shutting down. As worried as Americans were about terrorism or other foreign dangers, these concerns were swept to the side. The economy was faltering in ways not seen since the Great Depression of the 1930s. As the crisis progressed, hundreds of thousands of people were losing their jobs each month. Those who weren't facing unemployment themselves almost certainly knew someone who was. At the same time, a mortgage crisis eventually cut the value of the stock market by more than a third. People saw much of their savings and retirement accounts evaporate. This was both a frightening and a very immediate problem.

The economy was not an area where Senator McCain could boast of any special expertise. And he hurt his own cause in mid-September by announcing

THE GREAT DEPRESSION

The Great Depression (1929–1939) was a devastating economic downturn in the United States. At one point, one in four people was jobless, and many families were homeless.

that he believed the economy was in good shape. Obama, in contrast, projected a sober awareness of how serious the crisis was—and a willingness to take whatever steps were necessary to solve it.

The presidential debates were an opportunity for both candidates to convince undecided voters to make a commitment. In 2008, there were four debates in all, three between Obama and McCain and one between Senator Biden and Governor Palin. These events allowed the candidates to explain their views on a variety of topics, and sometimes to exchange opinions directly with each other.

Most viewers did not watch the debates expecting to hear truly new ideas that would convince them to support a candidate they hadn't been sure about before. The debates were more of an opportunity to see how a candidate stood up under pressure. Did he or she get flustered by an unexpected question? Did the candidate show a sense of humor?

On October 7, 2008, Senators Obama and McCain fielded questions from the audience in a "town hall" style debate.

Was there a perception that the candidate was comfortable in his own skin—not just trying to be all things to all people?

The 2008 debates were not a knockout for either side. However, in polls taken afterward, Obama was generally seen to have come across a little better, which was important since McCain was constantly trying to present Obama as an inexperienced leader, a man who would use the presidency for on-the-job training. But McCain failed to make this charge stick. And his continued attempts to do so only made him look desperate.

On November 3, the day before the election, Obama learned that his grandmother had died in Hawaii. Toot had been ill for some time, so her passing was not unexpected. Still, as the one remaining link to his childhood family, Obama had hoped Toot could see his quest fulfilled. As he had written earlier, it was his grandmother "whose dogged

Former secretary of state Colin Powell, a long-time Republican who had served several Republican presidents, appeared on talk shows to explain his endorsement of Senator Obama.

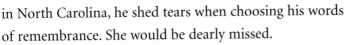

Barack and Michelle Obama clearly enjoyed their opportunity to vote on November 4, 2008.

practicality kept the family afloat" during his youth.

That afternoon, as he spoke briefly about his grandmother to a crowd in North Carolina, he shed tears when choosing his words of remembrance. She would be dearly missed.

On election day, November 4, Obama voted in Chicago. He had been leading in the polls for weeks, but nobody was ready to take a victory for granted. There was still some concern about the perceived gap between what people would say in public, and what they would do in the privacy of a voting booth. Would a majority of Americans truly put aside over 200 years of bias and bigotry to vote for a man with a background so different from their own?

That night, the question was answered. Although the predictions remained cautious through the early evening, Obama support held steady. Just after 11:00 PM in the east, the news outlets declared Obama the winner. And the victory wasn't concentrated only in traditional Democratic strongholds. For the first time in several elections, a Democrat had won traditionally Republican states such as Colorado and Indiana. Candidate Obama had won with 53 percent of the vote.

Electoral College

U.S. presidents are not elected by a direct, popular vote. As dictated by the Constitution, they are chosen by electors, a set number of representative voters for each state. This means that each state has a certain number of electoral votes (based on the number of representatives it has in congress). An electoral map (below) shows in red (Republican) and blue (Democrat) who has won each state, and the number of electors in each state. A candidate must win at least 270 of the 538 electoral votes available to become president.

The Obamas had been watching and waiting all night in a Chicago hotel room. Michelle's mother, Joe and Jill Biden, and a few close friends and campaign officials had joined them for parts of the evening. Malia and Sasha nervously watched the returns with their parents, dressed in fine dresses for the family appearance that would follow—whether their father won or not. But once the returns were in, the smiles returned to their faces. After midnight, the family went to Chicago's Grant Park, and President-elect Obama shared his thoughts:

If there is anyone out there who still doubts that America is a place where all things are possible, who still wonders if the dream of our founders is alive in our time, who still questions the power of our democracy, tonight is your answer.

This election had many firsts and many stories that will be told for generations. But one that's on my mind tonight's about a woman who cast her ballot in Atlanta. She's a lot like the millions of others who stood in line to make their voice heard in this election except for one thing: Ann Nixon Cooper is 106 years old. She was born just a generation past slavery; a time when there were no cars on the road or planes in the sky; when someone like her couldn't vote for two reasons—because she was a woman and because of the color of her skin . . .

America, we have come so far. We have seen so much. But there is so much more to do. So tonight, let us ask ourselves—if our children should live to see the next century; if my daughters should be so lucky to live as long as Ann Nixon Cooper, what change will they see? What progress will we have made?

This is our chance to answer that call.

It was truly a night to remember.

chapter **13**

Mr. President

O n the morning of January 20, 2009, Barack and Michelle Obama went to church. It was one of many inaugural traditions they would observe that day. Later that morning, they would have coffee at the White House with President and Mrs. Bush. Then there would be the procession to the Capitol, the swearing-in ceremony at noon, and a luncheon with all the members of Congress. The afternoon would be spent watching participants from all 50 states take part in the inaugural parade. Finally, the day would end long after dark, as the Obamas made appearances at a series of inaugural balls.

The White House, at 1600 Pennsylvania Avenue in Washington, D.C., has been home to all of the American presidents since 1800.

The Obama family had been staying at Blair House, a government-owned residence right across the street from the White House. Two weeks earlier, Malia and Sasha had started classes at their new school. The rest of the

Secretary of State

The secretary of state is the highest-ranking member of the presidential cabinet and the head of the Department of State. The secretary, under the president's direction, is in charge of all international political matters that concern or affect the United States.

settling-in would have to wait until the family moved into the White House that night.

Of course, Inauguration Day was only the latest in a series of busy days for President-elect Obama. For the two and a half months since election day, he and his staff had made many decisions concerning the shape of his administration. High among their priorities was filling important jobs at the top—the cabinet positions. The most notable selection involved his former opponent, Senator Hillary Clinton. Obama asked her to become secretary of state, an offer she proudly accepted.

Despite all the tough problems that lay ahead, this Tuesday was a time for celebration. And the highlight would clearly be the inaugural address. Every elected president had given this speech after taking the oath of office. Not that the speeches necessarily had much in common. In 135 polite but perfunctory words, George Washington's second inaugural address in 1793 was the shortest. William Henry Harrison

weighed in with more than 8,000 words in 1841. He spoke for about two hours and caught a cold in the wet weather. He never recovered, and died of pneumonia a month later.

President Obama had nothing either so long or short in mind. He hoped to strike a note of confidence in the future, even as the country was dealing with the toughest problems it had faced in generations: wars in Iraq and Afghanistan, long-standing uncertainties in the Middle East, and an economy that was severely damaged.

But Obama wanted to remind America that no problem is too big to overcome when its citizens all work together.

President-elect Obama took the oath of office from the chief justice of the U.S. Supreme Court, John Roberts, while his family looked on.

"Today I say to you that the challenges we face are real. They are serious and they are many. They will not be met easily or in a short span of time. But know this, America—they will be met. . . . Starting today, we must pick ourselves up, dust ourselves off, and begin again the work of remaking America."

After a childhood spent seeking a sense of his history and identity and an early career learning

The Obamas appeared at many inaugural balls on the evening after the new president was sworn in.

about the concerns of others, little Barry had grown into a man people around the world felt they knew. In fact,

Inaugural Addresses

Only a few inaugural addresses have included phrases that have been considered memorable. Besides presidents Kennedy and Lincoln, who are often cited for their eloquence, Thomas Jefferson set the tone for bringing the country together in 1801, stating that "every difference of opinion is not a difference of principle. We have called by different names brethren of the same principle. We are all Republicans, we are all Federalists." And in 1933, Franklin D. Roosevelt tried to reassure the country during the Great Depression, stating: "The only thing we have to fear is fear itself—nameless, unreasoning, unjustified terror which paralyzes needed efforts to convert retreat into advance."

President Obama met with Secretary of the State Hillary Clinton shortly after her appointment became official.

his inauguration was watched on television and heard on radios all over the globe. Kenya declared a national holiday in his honor. And President Obama had thoughts to share with his global audience, "from the grandest capitals to the small village where my father was born:

"What is required of us now is a new era of responsibility . . . This is the price and the promise of citizenship."

–Barack Obama, from his inaugural address

know that America is a friend of each nation and every man, woman, and child who seeks a future of peace and dignity, and we are ready to lead once more."

The weeks and months ahead would not be easy. "What is required of us now is a new era of responsibility—a recognition, on the part of every American, that we have duties to ourselves, our nation, and the world, duties that we do not grudgingly accept but rather seize gladly, firm in the knowledge that there is nothing so satisfying to the spirit, so defining of our character, than giving our all to a difficult task. . . . This is the price and the promise of citizenship."

As President Obama finished speaking, a wave of applause swept from the steps of the Capitol down the National Mall, where millions of people had come to witness this moment. No magic wand could sweep away the crises that the president and the country were now facing. As much as he might like to, the president could not predict with certainty what lay ahead for himself or his fellow Americans. But as he had shown many times before over the course of his life, he had hope and faith that the future would be a bright one.

President Obama boards his official helicopter, Marine One, on the way to Andrews Air Force Base.

Events in the Life of Barack Obama

Summer/Fall 1967
Ann marries Lolo Soetoro;
the family moves to
Jakarta in Indonesia.

August 4, 1961
Barack Obama is
born in Honolulu,
Hawaii, to Barack
Obama, Sr., and Ann
Dunham Obama.

September 1979
After graduation
from Punahou
School, Obama
enters Occidental
College in Los
Angeles, California.

June 1985
The new graduate moves to Chicago to
begin a job as a community organizer,
working with church-based groups in
urban neighborhoods.

Summer 1991
Obama graduates from
law school and moves
back to Chicago as a
civil rights lawyer.

Summer 1971
Obama returns to
Hawaii to live with his
grandparents, Stanley
and Madelyn Dunham.

January 1964
After a two-year
separation, Ann files for
divorce from Barack Sr.

June 1983
Obama graduates
from Columbia
and begins his
first job, as a
researcher in
New York City.

Summer 1988
Obama visits Kenya
and meets his
father's extended
family; enters
Harvard Law School.

August 1981
Obama transfers
to Columbia
University in New
York City, majoring
in political science.

Spring 1990
Obama becomes
the first African-
American president
of the *Harvard
Law Review*.

October 13, 1992
Barack Obama and Michelle Robinson are married.

July 27, 2004
Obama gives the keynote speech at the Democratic National Convention, where John Kerry is nominated as a presidential nominee.

November 2, 2004
Obama is elected to the U.S. Senate.

November 1996
Obama is elected to the Illinois state senate.

November 4, 2008
Obama defeats John McCain in the presidential election.

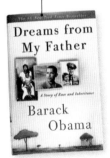

June 10, 2001
Natasha (Sasha) Obama is born.

January 20, 2009
Obama is inaugurated as the 44th president of the United States.

Fall 2000
Bobby Rush defeats Obama in the race for a seat in the U.S. House of Representatives.

June 1995
Dreams From My Father is published.

July 4, 1998
Malia Obama is born.

Bibliography

The Editors of LIFE. *The American Journey of Barack Obama.* New York: Little, Brown and Company, 2008.

Finnegan, William. "The Candidate." *The New Yorker,* May 31, 2004: http://www.newyorker.com/archive/2004/05/31/040531fa_fact1

Fornek, Scott and Dave McKinney. "Obama Makes It Official." *Chicago Sun Times,* February 11, 2007.

"How He Did It." *Newsweek,* November 5, 2008. http://www.newsweek.com/id/167582

Mendell, David. *Obama: From Promise to Power.* New York: HarperCollins, 2007.

Obama, Barack. 2004 Democratic Convention keynote speech, http://www.washingtonpost.com/wp-dyn/articles/A19751-2004Jul27.html

Obama, Barack. *The Audacity of Hope.* New York: Three Rivers Press, 2006.

Obama, Barack. "Barack Obama's Acceptance Speech." http://www.nytimes.com/2008/08/28/us/politics/28text-obama.html

Obama, Barack. *Dreams From My Father.* New York: Three Rivers Press, 1995.

Obama, Barack. "Full Text of Senator Barack Obama's Announcement for President." http://www.barackobama.com/2007/02/10/remarks_of_senator_barack_obam_11.php

Obama, Barack. "President Barack Obama's Inaugural Address." http://www.whitehouse.gov/blog/inaugural-address/

Obama, Barack. "Remarks of President-Elect Obama: Election Night." http://www.barackobama.com/2008/11/

Remini, Robert V. and Terry Golway, eds. *Fellow Citizens: The Penguin Book of U.S. Presidential Inaugural Addresses.* New York: Penguin Books, 2008.

Washington, James M., ed. *A Testament of Hope: The Essential Writings of Martin Luther King, Jr.* San Francisco: HarperCollins, 1991.

For Further Study

Dreams From My Father is Barack Obama's memoir about growing up, going to college, his first jobs, and visiting his ancestral home in Kenya.

This site is the political headquarters for Obama's political campaigns and a place to get involved in the his political organization: www.barackobama.com

The official White House website provides information about the White House and the current president, including recent news and initiatives: www.whitehouse.gov

The Biography website is a source for information about not only about Barack Obama, but also about many of the people who have been important in his political and personal life: www.biography.com/featured-biography/barack-obama

Works Cited

p.6: "Let the word go forth . . ." *Fellow Citizens*, p.386.

p.8: "Now is the time . . ." *A Testament of Hope*, p.217

p.13: "that my father . . ." *Dreams from My Father*, p.10.

p.13: "retrace the first steps. . ." ibid. p.23.

p.18: "a sleepy backwater . . ." *The Audacity of Hope*, p.273.

p.19: "dog meat . . ." ibid. p.37.

p.19: "One day soon . . ." ibid. p.37.

p.19: "Keep your ends up . . ." ibid. p.36.

p.20: "You want to keep . . ." ibid. p.37.

p.20: "If you can't . . ." ibid. p.41.

p.20: "a joyous time . . ." *The Audacity of Hope*, p.274.

p.21: "the face . . ." *Dreams from My Father*, p.37.

p.23: "This is no picnic . . ." ibid. p.48.

p.23: "She knew . . ." ibid. p.47.

p.25: "My grandfather . . ." ibid. p.63.

p.26: "Well . . . if I want to . . ." ibid. p.63.

p.26: "I had visions . . ." ibid. p.64.

p.27: "disdained any kind . . ." ibid. p.66.

p.27: "You have me . . ." ibid. p.50.

p.29: "He was much . . ." ibid. p.65.

p.30: "I doubted . . ." ibid. p.75.

p.30: "with a consuming . . ." ibid. p.78.

p.31: "respect came . . ." ibid. p.79.

p.31: "As it was . . ." ibid. p.82.

p.32: "I started . . ." ibid. p.67.

p.33: "slipped it . . ." ibid. p.95.

p.35: "I had nothing . . ." ibid. p.99.

p.35: "weren't defined . . ." ibid. p.99.

p.36: "Who told . . ." ibid. p.110.

p.37: "demands that . . ." ibid. p.106.

p.40: "I saw the . . ." ibid. p.134-135.

p.44: "stuff that. . ." ibid. p.158.

p.44: "a do-nothing . . ." ibid. p.155.

p.45: "In places . . ." ibid. p.252.

p.46: "But for the . . ." ibid. p.258.

p.50: "a new promised . . ." ibid. p.302.

p.52: "the Old Man's . . ." ibid. p.214.

p.54: "My family . . ." ibid. p.328.

p.54: "I am telling . . ." ibid. p.336

p.55: "the well-worn . . ." ibid. p.318.

p.59: "If I say . . ." ibid. p.371.

p.59: "I realized . . ." ibid. p.430.

p.63: "For someone . . ." *The Audacity of Hope*, p.331.

p.64: "tasted of . . ." ibid. p.330.

p.68: "the stripped-down . . ." ibid. p.84.

p.69: "honesty, empathy . . ." ibid. p.205.

p.69: "she had an . . ." ibid. p.205.

p.71: "a tradition . . ." ibid. p.2.

p.73: "I talked . . ." ibid. p.1.

p.75: "It was an . . ." ibid. p.3.

p.76: "I noticed that . . ." "The Candidate"

p.76: "I am not . . ." *The American Journey of Barack Obama*, p.67.

p.77: "a rash . . ." ibid. p.67

p.77: "to try out . . ." *The Audacity of Hope*, p.5.

p.79: "it sometimes . . ." ibid. p.68.

p.79: "If we . . ." ibid. p.68.

p.80: "They wanted . . ." ibid. p.7.

p.80: "They believed . . ." ibid. p.7.

p.82: "a faith in . . ." 2004 Democratic Convention keynote speech

p.83 : "hope in . . ." ibid.

p.85: "fierce . . ." *The Audacity of Hope*, p.18.

p.85: "made no effort . . ." ibid. p.210.

p.88: "I will be . . ." *The American Journey of Barack Obama*, p.69.

p.88: "Most people . . ." *The Audacity of Hope*, p.116.

p.89: "our democracy . . ." ibid. p.57.

p.90: "by nature . . ." ibid. p.21.

p.90: "When Democrats . . ." *The Audacity of Hope*, p.21.

p.91: "I've never . . ." ibid. p.116.

p.92: "I am not running . . ." "Obama Makes It Official"

p.95: "Are you going . . ." *The American Journey of Barack Obama*, p.123.

p.97: "What's stopped us . . ." "Full Text of Senator Barack Obama's Announcement for President"

p.97: "But through his. . ." ibid.

p.101: "The profound . . ." *The American Journey of Barack Obama*, p.105.

p.103: "Tonight, more . . ." "Barack Obama's Acceptance Speech"

p.104: "Tough luck . . . " ibid.

p.105: "Protect us . . ." ibid.

p.105: "in America . . ." ibid.

p.113: "whose dogged . . ." *The Audacity of Hope*, p.346.

p.115: "If there is . . ." "Remarks of president-Elect Obama: Election Night"

p.119: "Today I . . ." "President Barack Obama's Inaugural Address"

p.119: "Every difference . . ." *Fellow Citizens*, p.23

p.119: "The only thing . . ." ibid. p.334

p.120: ". . . from the grandest . . ." "President Barack Obama's Inaugural Address"

p.120: "What is required . . ." ibid.

Index

Acknowledgments

My thanks to my editor Beth Hester for her helpful comments throughout the writing process and to my agent Susie Cohen for her usual, but much appreciated, attention to detail.

Picture Credits

Front Cover Photo by Corbis/Ron Sachs. **Back Cover Photo** by DK Images.

The photographs in this book are used with permission and through the courtesy of:

DK Images: pp. 1, 11, 16T, 16–17B, 52, 56T, 86, 97 all, 109L. **Official Senate Photo:** pp. 2–3, 94, 123BR. **Getty Images:** pp. 5, 90 Congressional Quarterly; pp. 18, 28, 46–47, 53, 58, 79, 87, 99B, 106, 107, 108, 112, 122TR, 123TC Getty Images; p. 19 Gail Shumway; pp. 22–23 Dave Hamman; p. 55 Nicholas Parfitt; pp. 56–57 Harald Sund; p. 83 AFP; p. 96 WireImage. **JFK Library:** p. 6. **Library of Congress:** pp. 9, 98, 114. **Corbis:** pp. 10, 29 Obama for America; p. 14 Robert Harding World Imagery/Fraser Hall; p. 26 Chinch Gryniewicz; p. 38 Lee Snider; p. 71 Kevin Burke; p. 80 Kenneth Dickerman; p. 82 Rick Wilking/Reuters; pp. 85, 123TR John Gress/Reuters; p. 101 Eric Schlegee; p. 104–105, 118 Ralf-Finn Hestoff; p. 111 Matthew Cavanaugh; p. 119 Mark Wilson; p. 120 Pete Souza/White House; p. 121 Shawn Thew. **Polaris Images:** pp. 12, 13, 15, 21, 31, 32, 33, 54, 60, 63, 64, 109R, 122TL&BL. **Associated Press:** pp. 24, 42, 43, 48, 49, 74, 75, 84, 113. **Obama for America:** pp. 25, 45, 67T, B, 76, 123TL, 123BLC. **Ambient Images:** pp. 34, 36. **2004–2007 Landov:** p. 41 Obama for America; p. 73 Frank Polich; p. 89 Roger Wollenberg; p. 99T Brian Kersey; p. 103 Kevin Dietsch. **Alamy Images:** p. 51 Peter Jordan. **Harvard Law Review Association and William S. Hein Company/Vol.122, no. 7:** p. 61. **Harvard University:** pp. 65, 122BR. **White House:** p. 68. **Marc PoKempner:** p. 72. **Aurora Images:** p. 93 Callie Shell. **Destination DC:** p. 116 Mary A. Behre.

BORDER IMAGES from left to right: Harvard University; Destination DC/Mary A. Behre; Obama for America; Obama for America; DK Images; White House Photo

About the Author

Stephen Krensky is the author of more than 100 fiction and nonfiction books for children, including *DK Biography: Benjamin Franklin* and works on George Washington, the Wright Brothers, and the invention of the printing press. He lives in Lexington, Massachusetts, with his wife, Joan, and their family.

Other DK Biographies you'll enjoy:

Abigail Adams
Kem Knapp Sawyer
ISBN 978-0-7566-5209-8 paperback
ISBN 978-0-7566-5208-1 hardcover

Marie Curie
Vicki Cobb
ISBN 978-0-7566-3831-3 paperback
ISBN 978-0-7566-3832-0 hardcover

Charles Darwin
David C. King
ISBN 978-0-7566-2554-2 paperback
ISBN 978-0-7566-2555-9 hardcover

Princess Diana
Joanne Mattern
ISBN 978-0-7566-1614-4 paperback
ISBN 978-0-7566-1613-7 hardcover

Amelia Earhart
Tanya Lee Stone
ISBN 978-0-7566-2552-8 paperback
ISBN 978-0-7566-2553-5 hardcover

Thomas Edison
Jan Adkins
ISBN 978-0-7566-5207-4 paperback
ISBN 978-0-7566-5206-7 hardcover

Albert Einstein
Frieda Wishinsky
ISBN 978-0-7566-1247-4 paperback
ISBN 978-0-7566-1248-1 hardcover

Benjamin Franklin
Stephen Krensky
ISBN 978-0-7566-3528-2 paperback
ISBN 978-0-7566-3529-9 hardcover

Gandhi
Amy Pastan
ISBN 978-0-7566-2111-7 paperback
ISBN 978-0-7566-2112-4 hardcover

Harry Houdini
Vicki Cobb
ISBN 978-0-7566-1245-0 paperback
ISBN 978-0-7566-1246-7 hardcover

Thomas Jefferson
Jacqueline Ching
ISBN 978-0-7566-4506-9 paperback
ISBN 978-0-7566-4505-2 hardcover

Helen Keller
Leslie Garrett
ISBN 978-0-7566-0339-7 paperback
ISBN 978-0-7566-0488-2 hardcover

Joan of Arc
Kathleen Kudlinksi
ISBN 978-0-7566-3526-8 paperback
ISBN 978-0-7566-3527-5 hardcover

John F. Kennedy
Howard S. Kaplan
ISBN 978-0-7566-0340-3 paperback
ISBN 978-0-7566-0489-9 hardcover

Martin Luther King, Jr.
Amy Pastan
ISBN 978-0-7566-0342-7 paperback
ISBN 978-0-7566-0491-2 hardcover

Abraham Lincoln
Tanya Lee Stone
ISBN 978-0-7566-0834-7 paperback
ISBN 978-0-7566-0833-0 hardcover

Nelson Mandela
Lenny Hort & Laaren Brown
ISBN 978-0-7566-2109-4 paperback
ISBN 978-0-7566-2110-0 hardcover

Mother Teresa
Maya Gold
ISBN 978-0-7566-3880-1 paperback
ISBN 978-0-7566-3881-8 hardcover

Annie Oakley
Chuck Wills
ISBN 978-0-7566-2997-7 paperback
ISBN 978-0-7566-2986-1 hardcover

Pelé
Jim Buckley
ISBN 978-0-7566-2987-8 paperback
ISBN 978-0-7566-2996-0 hardcover

Eleanor Roosevelt
Kem Knapp Sawyer
ISBN 978-0-7566-1496-6 paperback
ISBN 978-0-7566-1495-9 hardcover

Harriet Tubman
Kem Knapp Sawyer
ISBN 978-0-7566-5806-9 paperback
ISBN 978-0-7566-5807-6 hardcover

George Washington
Lenny Hort
ISBN 978-0-7566-0835-4 paperback
ISBN 978-0-7566-0832-3 hardcover

Laura Ingalls Wilder
Tanya Lee Stone
ISBN 978-0-7566-4508-3 paperback
ISBN 978-0-7566-4507-6 hardcover